Do-It-Yourself Decorating

Step-by-Step
Pillows & Cushions

Hilary More

Meredith® Books

Des Moines, Iowa

Contents

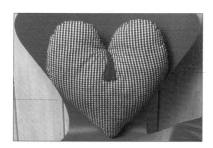

Floor and Seating Cushions   56

Hand-Stitched Cushions   66

Sewing Techniques   80

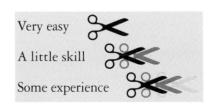

Very easy

A little skill

Some experience

Before You Begin

Cushions usually are the final addition to a room's decor. But before you stitch up a couple of plain, square covers, think about how your whole scheme can be transformed with a bit of imagination.

Mix and match interesting shapes and unusual fabrics. For example, because scatter cushions don't receive much wear and tear, make them from dressmaking fabrics, rather than soft furnishing material. Different fillers give you additional options, too. Choose from a range that includes solid foam for cushions that need to fit into shaped seats and soft feathers for those that are tossed onto beds or sofas. Whatever type of cushions you decide to make, remember that there is a wide range of materials available to foster your creativity.

Fabric colors and designs

Color and design decisions are important choices that will have a big impact on your room's decor. When it comes to thinking about color schemes for your cushions, keep in mind that the smallest cushions impact a room with their color: a group of bright-hued cushions relieve a large neutral expanse, while a range of subtle-toned cushions quiet down and harmonize even the most exuberant interior.

MIXING AND MATCHING

▼ ► Never be afraid to use color. It's easy to mix and match different shades, and by following a few straightforward rules, you will find yourself creating some delightful decorative schemes. It's helpful if you begin by thinking of colors in terms of groupings. The simplest approach is to split them into two basic categories—neutral shades and true colors.

WORKING WITH NEUTRAL SHADES

▲ Neutral shades often are the basis for a sophisticated and engaging room. Using textured fabrics—from those with subtle sheen to nubby and heavily woven fabrics—can enhance this look.

WORKING WITH TRUE COLORS

◄ Closely related, harmonious colors provide an appealing cushion selection.

To create successful schemes, think of the arrangement of colors on the color wheel. Like the rainbow, this wheel is made up of red, orange, yellow, green, blue, and violet.

◄ Contrasting colors lie directly opposite each other on the color wheel. Adding accents of contrasting color with scatter cushions could bring your decor to life; even a contrasting ruffle or piping can lift your color scheme, too.

Look closely at different patterned fabrics to see how designers use contrasting colors to breathe life into a particular design. Fabric collections often have designs in bright tones of harmonious shades as well as designs with contrasting touches.

MAKING YOUR CHOICES

Once you decide on your color preferences, collect samples of the colors and designs that appeal to you. Take the samples to the fabric store and select swatches of material that contain these features. Bring the swatches home to see for yourself just how certain combinations work together.

Another option is to buy enough fabric to make one small cushion cover and set it in a sofa or chair to gauge how the fabric looks in sunlight and artificial light. Once you settle on a suitable color scheme, plan the shape and style of the cushions so they enhance your particular scheme (see pages 8 and 9)

DESIGN MOTIFS

Unless the cushion's edge is broken by a ruffle or piping, patterns should generally be centered on cushion fronts and backs and matched so that they meet at the side seams. Be wary of large motifs, unless you are making extra-large cushions.

HOT AND COLD

▼ Colors also can be divided into hot colors (red, orange, and yellow) and cool colors (green, blue, and violet).

▼ Use cushions to advance the climate of a room. Try hot-colored cushions to add warmth in cold, north-facing rooms. Use cool colors to give the room a fresh, soothing feel.

Shapes and styles

Before you decide on the shape and style of your cushions, consider the following: First, think about the style and design of your apartment or house. Then, consider the style of the rest of the furnishings. Finally, think about your reasons for adding cushions. For assistance, look through magazines and visit show rooms for ways to use cushions as style pointers in different rooms.

STYLE POINTERS

▲ Different shapes and styles can look quite dramatic when placed together in a room. However, it may take considerable confidence and practice to achieve this with real flair. You might want to start out with more modest experiments, such as adding creative trims, pleats, and tucks.

CONTRASTS

▲ As a general principle, modern interiors with minimalist-style furniture are best enhanced with small cushions in clean-cut shapes made from crisp linens or well-pressed, semi-textured fabrics. A formal decor will benefit from more luxurious, larger-scale designs.

ON THE RIGHT SCALE

◄ Dimension is an important factor when fitting cushions into a decor. Overcrowding sofas and chairs with larger-than-life cushions only reduces the seating space, while delicate cushions placed on large, streamlined sofas look lost and out of proportion. Before you cut out the main fabric, consider making up a series of cushion forms (see page 11) and leave them scattered in the areas you wish to accentuate. The scale as well as the shape is important, as one dominant cushion tends to add dimension.

STYLED THEMES

▲ For Oriental schemes, arrange cushions featuring single-color prints against an open, spacious background with uncluttered lines. Brightly colored cushions are usually at home with any decor, as long as they are dressed up in an eye-catching print.

TAKING SHAPE

▲ It can be fun to design your own shape, as long as the outline is not too complicated. Simply enlarge your design outline on a photocopier and cut this out twice in fabric. Add gussets to give reinforcement to cushion shapes, particularly those used to pad seats and benches.

Fabric types, forms, and fillers

Cushion covers can be created with almost any type of fabric, but it is probably best to avoid especially fine or loosely-woven materials. Because covers generally need frequent laundering, the best fabric choices often belong to the cotton-based families. Select tough, hard-wearing fabrics such as closely woven cottons, linens, and cotton/polyester mixes. In general, avoid bulky fabrics that are difficult to sew and any fabrics requiring professional laundering and pressing.

EXCEPTIONS TO THE RULE

Tough cottons and cotton/synthetic mixes may be especially good choices for cushion covers, but you probably will want more leeway than this. If you choose to use a delicate fabric, try fixing it to a backing of plain, fine cotton. Totally synthetic fabrics, such as glitzy metallic materials, aren't always desirable from the washing point of view, but they may be just the thing to liven up your decor. These are best used on a small surface area of a cushion. Similarly, precious remnants that you've purchased and saved—particularly ones that are too expensive to use over any large area—may be perfect for cushions.

NATURAL OR SYNTHETIC?

Fibers used in home furnishing fabrics generally fall into two categories: natural and synthetic. Natural fibers—wool, linen, cotton, and silk—clean well, although they can shrink and wrinkle. Synthetic fabrics—rayon and viscose—may not be as aesthetically pleasing, but they often wash well, keep their shape, and are crease-resistant. Happily, manufacturers have now combined natural and synthetic fibers that offer the best of both worlds.

CUSHION FORMS

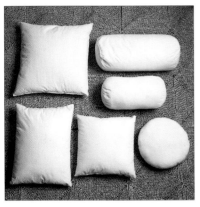

Cushions need a substantial form to prolong their life and maintain their shape. Choose your style, shape, outer fabric, and then consider the form.

A good range of cushion forms is available on the market, offering many popular shapes in a wide selection of sizes. For example, square cushion forms range from 8×8 inches to 30×30 inches.

If you are making a cushion in an unusual size or want to use a particular filler, stitch your own form. Form covers can be sewn from a variety of inexpensive fabrics, including calico, ticking, and lining fabric. For long life, choose hard-wearing, firm-woven cotton. Feather-filled forms should be made using down-proof fabrics. These are made with a special finish that helps prevent feathers from working through the fabric.

CUSHION FILLERS

When choosing your filler, consider the placement of the cushion and how much wear it should expect. The different types are:

Feathers

This is a favorite filler for bed cushions. Feathers are often mixed with down to produce a soft, luxurious cushion, needing only a quick shake to retain its desired shape.

Kapok

This is a soft, inexpensive vegetable filler used in the past for mattresses and sleeping bags. Forms stuffed with kapok eventually will lose their shape.

Synthetic fibers

These fillers are inexpensive, washable, hypo-allergenic, and can be covered with cotton or calico. They come packaged in bags or in sheets of batting of various thicknesses.

Foam

Foam is available as chips, shredded, or in blocks and is a particularly good choice for outdoor cushions. Foam chips and shredded foam provide cheap, non-absorbent fillers, but they can be lumpy, so wrap the form in a layer of batting to smooth the outline before fitting it inside the cover. Block foam is ideal for boxy shapes, but it is difficult to cut. If you bring your pattern to a fabric store, a clerk may be willing to cut it for you. To cut it yourself, use a bread knife and a back-and-forth sawing motion.

Plastic-foam beads or pellets

Small, expanded plastic-foam beads provide a good filler for floor cushions and bean bags because they make the cushions light to lift. The beads move about, molding to the contours of the sitter and producing a comfortable seat.

Simple Cushions

Sofas piled high with simple cushions in assorted colors and patterns always look inviting. Basic cushion covers are easy to make and require minimal fabric. To coordinate them with existing furnishings, use fabric left over from upholstery covers and curtains, or use small, treasured pieces of fabric.

If you want a change from square and rectangular shapes, you'll find round cushions, hearts, triangles, bolsters, even alphabet letters add interest and fun. You also have a selection when it comes to fastening methods, including slip-stitches, ties, vents, zippers, and hook-and-loop fastening tape. Your pillow design and shape will help determine the most suitable closure.

Basic covers and forms

Basic cushion covers consist simply of two fabric shapes sewn together with a slip-stitched opening placed centrally along one edge. Ready-made cushion forms are available in a good selection of sizes, but by producing your own you can make non-standard size cushions, just perfect for a treasured piece of cloth. To make a cushion form, choose down-proof ticking, cambric, calico, curtain lining, sheeting, or a similar closely woven cotton fabric.

MATERIALS: *Basic square cushion cover, 16×16 inches:* ½ yard of 45-inch-wide furnishing fabric, 16×16-inch cushion form, matching thread, tape measure, scissors, pins, needles
Basic square cushion form, 16×16 inches: ½ yard of 36-inch-wide fabric suitable for chosen filler (feathers or polyester), matching thread, tape measure, scissors, pins, needles

FABRIC: *Cushion cover, front and back:* Cut two squares of fabric, 1¼ inches wider and longer than the desired cushion size.
Cushion form, front and back: Cut two squares of fabric, 1¼ inches wider and longer than desired cushion size.

BASIC SQUARE COVER

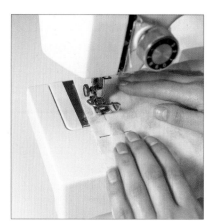

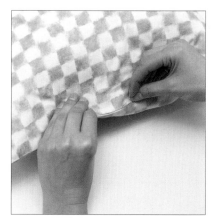

1 Join cushion cover back and front with right sides facing and matching raw edges. Pin, baste, and stitch pieces together using a ⅝-inch seam allowance. Sew around the four corners and three sides, leaving a center opening in remaining side. Backstitch at the beginning and end of the seam to secure stitches.

2 Trim the corners diagonally, cutting ⅛ inch from the stitching. Press open the seam allowance on each side of the opening and the seam allowance on the opening. Turn the cover right side out, pulling out the corners. Press the cover flat, with the seams at the exact edge of the cushion cover.

3 Insert the cushion form. Pin the cover opening together and use slip-stitches to close it. Create rectangular covers (and forms) in the same manner as for the square covers, positioning the opening centrally in one short side. For a 14×18-inch cushion, you will need ½ yard of 45-inch-wide fabric.

CUSHION FORMS

Make up a cushion form in the same way as a cover, leaving an opening in one side. Insert the filler, using a large-gauge knitting needle or wooden spoon handle to work it well into the corners. Instead of slip-stitching the opening closed, machine stitch it to hold the filler firmly in place.

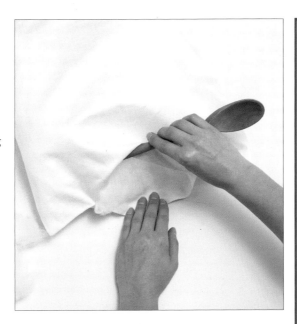

TIDY CORNERS

To eliminate wrinkled corners on plain square and rectangular cushion covers, sew around the corners in a curve. The degree of the curve will depend on the size of the cover.

1 Fold the piece of fabric for the front cover into quarters. Mark halfway between the fold and the corner on each open side. Mark ⅝ inch in from the corner point. Now draw a line around the corner in a gentle curve, from the center marks through the corner mark.

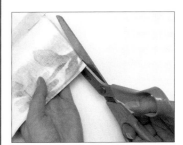

2 Keeping the fabric cover folded in quarters, cut along the marked line. Use the front as a pattern to cut out the back cover. Then stitch up a basic cushion cover, following steps 1–3 on page 14.

Interesting shapes

Cushions can be made in any shape, provided the outline isn't too complicated. First, draw an outline of your shape, smoothing out any over-complicated areas. Use a photocopier to enlarge the design to the chosen size and check that the shape is still recognizable. Cut out the pattern. If it's an unusual shape, you will need to make your own form. Do this first, to establish whether or not the pattern will work.

MATERIALS: *Round cushion, 12 inches in diameter:* ½ yard of 45-inch-wide furnishing fabric, same-size cushion form, matching thread, paper, pencil, string, push pin or tack, large cork tile or a clean, wooden chopping board, tape measure, scissors, pins, needles
Heart cushion, approximately 15×15 inches: ½ yard of 45-inch-wide furnishing fabric, same-size cushion form, graph paper, pencil, matching thread, tape measure, scissors, pins, needles

FABRIC: *Round cushion, front and back:* Measure the diameter of the form and add a ⅝-inch seam allowance all around to give the size for the front and back.
Heart cushion, front and back: Draw up a pattern (see Step 1 on page 17) and use this pattern to cut out two pieces from your fabric, adding ⅝ inch for a seam allowance all around the outer edge.

ROUND CUSHION COVER

1 For best results, make a paper pattern. Cut a square of paper slightly larger than the cutting size of the circle. Fold the square into quarters. Now cut a length of string about 8 inches longer than the radius of the circle. Tie one end around the pointed end of a pencil. Insert a push pin through the opposite end so that the distance between the two equals the radius of the circle. Place the paper pattern on a cork tile or chopping board and anchor the push pin into the folded corner. Holding the string taut, draw across the paper from edge to edge.

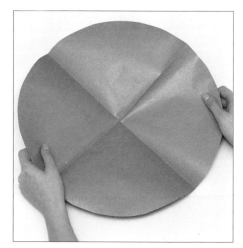

2 Keeping the paper folded, cut along the marked outline. Unfold the paper and use the pattern to cut a front and back, adding ⅝-inch seam allowances. If the fabric has a large motif, center motif on both pieces.

3 Place front and back together with right sides facing and outer edges matching. Pin, baste, and stitch two-thirds of the way around the outer edge, using a ⅝-inch seam allowance. Backstitch at either end of the seam to secure the stitches. Clip into the seam allowance at regular intervals around the circle.

4 Turn the cover right side out. Press so the seam is directly at the outer edge. Press the seam allowance to the inside at the opening. Insert cushion form and slip-stitch the opening closed.

HEART CUSHION COVER

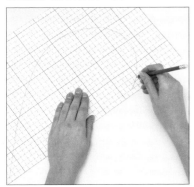

1 Fold a piece of graph paper in half lengthwise. Draw half of a heart motif, using the fold of the paper as the heart's center. Keeping the paper folded, cut out your outline. Unfold the paper and check the shape and size. Adjust as necessary.

2 Use the pattern to cut out a cushion front and back, adding a ⅝-inch seam allowance all around. Place front and back together with right sides facing and outer edges matching. Pin, baste, and stitch, leaving an opening at the bottom of one side edge. Backstitch at the beginning and end of the seam to secure the stitches.

3 Clip into the seam allowance all around the shape, then turn the cover right side out. Press the seam allowance to the inside on the opening, then press around the shape so the seam is at the outer edge. Make up a form and insert. Slip-stitch opening closed and add decorations, such as the tassel shown here.

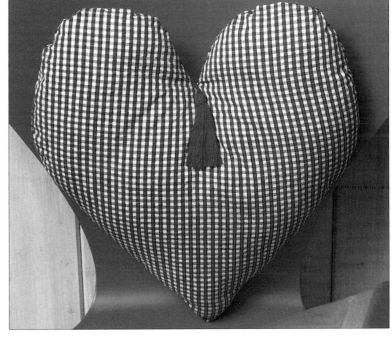

Bolsters

Bolsters have crisp edges and a long opening in the seam on the center section, making these covers easy to remove for cleaning. Choose between a softer style where the ends are gathered and accented with a large, self-covered button and a more tailored look edged with piping. Ready-made bolster forms come in a range of sizes. Or, you can make your own by following the instructions for the tailored bolster on page 19 (machine-stitch the opening closed after the filler is added instead of closing it with a zipper or slip-stitches).

MATERIALS: *Gathered bolster, 18 inches long with 7-inch-diameter ends:* ½ yard of 45-inch-wide furnishing fabric, same-size bolster form, two 1½-inch-diameter self-cover buttons and contrasting fabric for covering them, matching thread, tape measure, scissors, pins, needles
Tailored bolster, 18 inches long with 7-inch-diameter ends: ½ yard of 55-inch-wide furnishing fabric, same-size bolster form, 2½ yards of piping cord, matching thread, tape measure, scissors, paper, compass, pins, needles

FABRIC: *Gathered bolster, length:* Measure the length of the form, seam to seam. Measure the diameter of the end. Add both measurements together, then add 1¼ inches (for ⅝-inch seam allowances). *Depth:* Measure the circumference of the form and add 1¼ inches (for ⅝-inch seam allowances). Cut out one piece of fabric to this size.
Tailored bolster, center section: Measure the length of the form and add 1¼ inches (for ⅝-inch seam allowances). Measure form's circumference and add seam allowances. Cut one rectangle of fabric to this size. *Ends:* Measure diameter of one end of the bolster form and divide by two. On paper, draw a circle with the compass set to this measurement. Cut out pattern, adding ⅝-inch seam allowances, then cut two ends from fabric.

GATHERED BOLSTER

1 Fold fabric in half lengthwise with right sides together and raw edges matching. Using ⅝ inch for a seam allowance, pin, baste, and stitch along the long edge, forming a tube. Neaten both raw edges with zigzag stitches and press the seam open.

2 Turn the cover right side out. Press under raw edges at each end ⅝ inch. Using a double thread, work large, evenly-spaced gathering stitches around each pressed edge. Do not pull up gathers and leave the gathering thread on the needle.

3 Insert the bolster form into the cushion cover, centering it inside. At each end, pull up the gathering threads to close the end and fasten off the thread.

4 Cover each button with contrasting or matching fabric, (see Covering Buttons, below). Hand stitch the covered button over each gathered end to neaten.

TAILORED BOLSTER

1 Fold center section in half lengthwise with right sides together and matching raw edges. Using a ⅝-inch seam allowance, pin, baste, and stitch along the long edge, forming a tube, and leave an opening in the center of the seam. Leave the opening unstitched or insert a zipper (see pages 20 and 21).

2 Open the zipper, if necessary. Add piping cord around ends (see pages 32 and 33). With right sides together, pin, baste, and stitch an end circle to each open end of the center section. Clip into seam allowance and trim seams. Turn cover right side out, insert form, and close the opening.

COVERING BUTTONS

Follow the manufacturer's instructions for covering buttons. Use a guide to cut a circle of your chosen fabric. Run a gathering thread around the outer edge; gather covering around the button front and fasten. Ease fabric evenly around the outer edge of the button front and snap on the back.

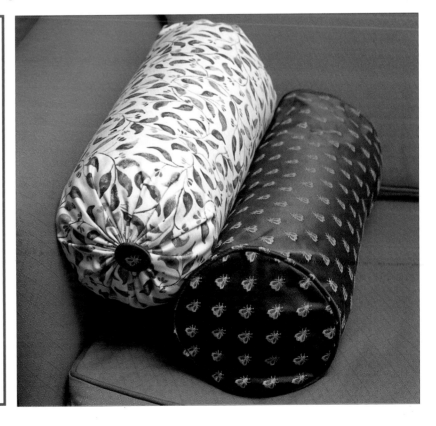

Fastenings

Fastenings for cushion covers can be as varied as the covers themselves. Usually an opening is placed along one edge or centered vertically or horizontally across the back. The easiest fastenings include slip-stitching the opening, forming an overlapping vent, and making an envelope-style opening with button-and-tie closures. More complicated options are zippers and hook-and-loop fastening tape. Lapped zippers are placed in a seam of the cover—preferably the bottom seam—while those inserted in a back seam generally are centered. Hook-and-loop fastening tapes generally are stitched into seam allowances. While this is easy enough to do, it does require a bit of know-how (and a double hem) to keep the stitches from showing on the right side. It's all explained here.

OVERLAPPING VENT

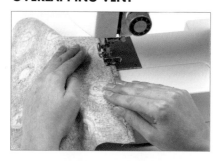

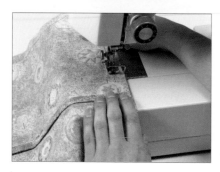

1 Cut out the cushion back, making it 4½ inches wider than the cushion front to create a 2¾-inch vertical overlap at the back of the cushion. Fold the back in half vertically and cut along the fold. Press under a ⅜-inch hem twice, down the center back edges of each back section. Pin, baste, then stitch the hems in place.

2 Place cushion backs right side up, overlapping center hem edges 2¾ inches. Secure the center edges temporarily with diagonal basting stitches.

3 Place the back and front together with right sides facing and matching outer edges. Pin, baste, and stitch using a ⅝-inch seam allowance. Turn right side out. Insert form.

CENTER SEAM ZIPPER

1 Choose a zipper 2 to 4 inches shorter than the cushion width. Place the two back cover pieces with right sides facing and raw edges matching. Pin and baste together along the center edge, using a ⅝-inch seam allowance. Mark the zipper length, centered, across the basted seam. Stitch from each side, up to the marks, working a few backstitches at each side to secure. Press seam open.

2 With the right side of the fabric down, place the zipper, also right side down, over the seam. Position the teeth centered over the basted section of the seam. Pin and baste in place.

3 Turn the fabric right side up and stitch all around the zipper. Remove basting threads and open zipper. Assemble the cover.

LAPPED ZIPPER

1 Select a zipper 2 to 4 inches shorter than the cushion side edge. Place back and front pieces with right sides facing and raw edges matching. Pin and baste the side seam.

Mark the zipper length, centered, on the basted seam. Stitch in from each side, up to the marks, using a ⅝-inch seam allowance and working a few backstitches to fasten. Press the seam open.

2 Open zipper and place it right side down on the front seam allowance only, with zipper teeth against the seam line; pin and baste. Using a zipper foot, machine-stitch zipper to seam allowance only.

3 Close zipper. Spread the cover flat, right sides up, covering the zipper teeth with the back seam allowance. Pin, baste, and stitch the zipper in place ⅜ inch from the seam line.

Open the zipper. Refold the cover with right sides facing. Stitch remaining sides. Turn right side out.

HOOK-AND-LOOP FASTENING TAPE

1 Turn under a double hem width on the opening edge of each piece; press and pin. Mark each end of the center opening with a pin.

2 Separate the two halves of the tape. With right side of fabric up, unfold the first fold of the hem. Pin one piece of tape centered over the double thickness of material. Stitch around the edges. Repeat for the other cover piece. Make sure the two halves match up before stitching the cover.

3 Refold the double hems and pin in place. Place the cover pieces right sides together and stitch in from each side edge, stopping ⅜ inch from the end of the fastening tape. Work a few backstitches to secure the stitches. Pin, baste, and stitch the remaining three sides, catching the folded hems.

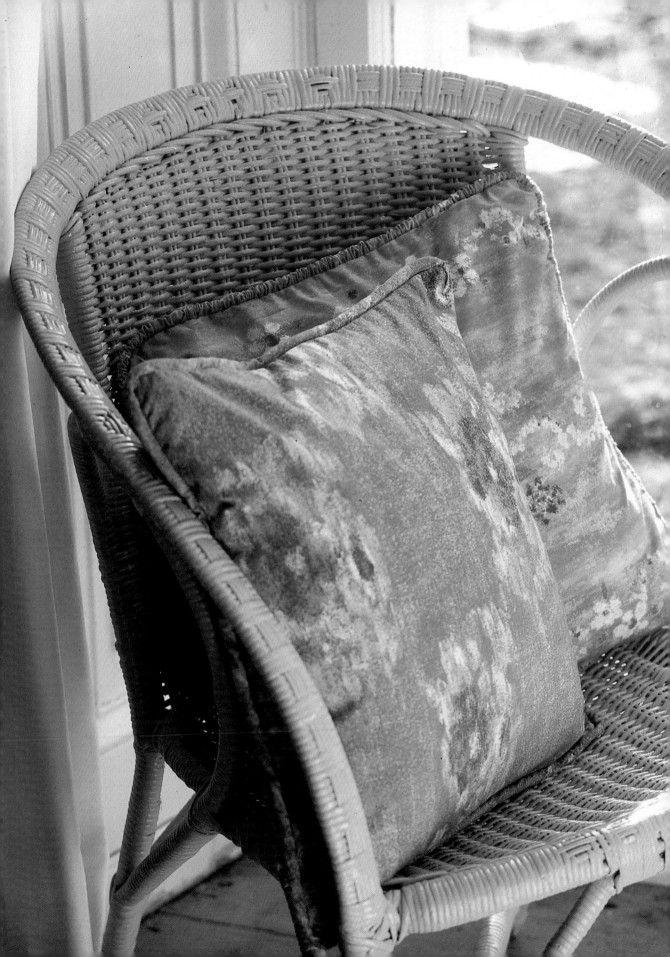

Decorative Finishes

Find the perfect match for your stitching skills, schedule, and sense of style by choosing from the huge variety of decorative finishes and fastenings in this chapter. Here is an area where you can give your imagination free rein. A single border provides a distinctive edge, while double borders and ruffles are easy ways to create a luxurious effect. The plainest cover is transformed with the addition of piping around the edges. (The piping not only accentuates the outline, it gives the cushion longer life, too.) And the stunning range of braids, cords, and trims on the market lends a touch of class to any cushion. Decoration need not be fussy or complicated either. One appealing option is to turn a cushion's fastening, such as ties or buttons, into an outstanding feature.

This chapter contains

Borders

A border is easy and lends a special touch to your cushion. Single-bordered cushions are stitched together before an integral border is formed with topstitching all around the outer edge. Double borders give an even more luxurious look. This mitered, double border is created on the front and back cushion pieces before they are stitched together.

MATERIALS: *Cushion with a 2½-inch-wide single border, 16×16 inches:* ¾ yard of 55-inch-wide furnishing fabric, 16×16-inch square cushion form, matching thread, tape measure, scissors, pins, needles
Cushion with a 2-inch-wide double border, 16×16 inches: ¾ yard of 55-inch-wide furnishing fabric, 16×16-inch square cushion form, matching thread, tape measure, scissors, pins, needles

FABRIC: *Cushion with 2½-inch-wide single border, front and back:* Measure width and length of the form, adding twice the width of the border plus 1¼ inches (for ⅝-inch seam allowances) to each measurement.
Cushion with 2-inch-wide double border, front: Measure the width and length of the form and add an extra 9 inches to both measurements for the border and seam allowances. *Back:* Cut one piece of fabric the same size as the front, adding an extra 1¼-inch seam allowance to one measurement for a center back opening.

SINGLE BORDER

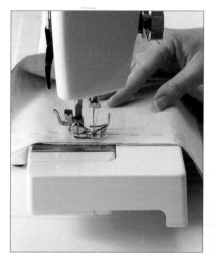

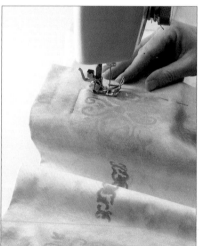

1 Place the front and back cover pieces with the right sides facing and raw edges matching. Pin, baste, and stitch, leaving an opening for inserting the form. Turn right side out and press.

2 Pin, baste, and machine-stitch around the cover again at the chosen border width, leaving a gap in the stitching that corresponds with the main opening.

3 Insert the form. Pin the outer opening closed. Using a piping foot, stitch across the inner gap, matching up with the previous stitching. Slip-stitch the outer opening closed.

DOUBLE BORDER

1 Insert a fastening in the center back seam or form a center opening that can be slip-stitched closed. Lay the back cover piece with the wrong side up. On all four sides, fold over the border width plus a ⅝-inch seam allowance. Press firmly. Repeat for the front cover.

2 Open the folded border and press in each corner until the pressed lines at a corner match the pressed lines along edges of cover. Press the diagonal fold.

3 Open the first corner. With right sides together, fold the corner in half diagonally, matching the outer edges. Stitch across the corner along the pressed diagonal fold line, forming a mitered corner. Trim the seam allowance and press open. Repeat with each corner.

4 Turn each corner right side out and press flat. Then repeat this process to form mitered corners on the front cover piece.

5 Place the front and the back pieces together with the wrong sides facing, matching the mitered corners. Pin, baste, and stitch the pieces together at the chosen border width, leaving an opening to insert the form. Insert the form, then sew the opening closed using slip-stitches.

Fancy ruffles

Ruffled cushions always look extravagant. A ruffle strip generally is cut 1½ to two times the perimeter of the cushion, but this depends on the required fullness and the weight of the fabric. (The heavier the fabric, the softer the gathers.) Ruffles usually are gathered, but they also can be pleated or gathered only at the corners. Single ruffles are cut with the straight grain of the fabric width and hemmed along one edge. A double ruffle, made from a strip of fabric folded in half, provides a more substantial border. It drapes best when cut on the fabric's bias.

MATERIALS: *Round cushion, 15 inches in diameter, with a 3-inch-wide single ruffle:* ¾ yard of 55-inch-wide furnishing fabric, 15-inch-diameter cushion form, matching thread, tape measure, scissors, pins, needles *Square cushion, 18×18 inches, with a 4-inch-wide double ruffle:* ¾ yard of 55-inch-wide furnishing fabric, 18×18-inch square cushion form, matching thread, tape measure, scissors, pins, needles

FABRIC: *Round cushion, front and back:* Measure across the form and add 1¼ inches (for ⅝-inch seam allowances). Cut two circles of fabric (see page 16). For a center-back opening, use half of the circle pattern, adding ⅝ inch to the straight edge for the seam allowance. Cut two patterns for the back. *Ruffle:* Measure the circumference of the form, then multiply this measurement 1½ to 2 times. Decide on the width of the ruffle and add 1⅜ inches (for a double ⅜-inch hem and a ⅝-inch seam allowance). Cut strips the width of the fabric and piece together until they are the desired length. *Square cushion, front and back:* Measure the width and length of the form and add 1¼ inches to each measurement (for ⅝-inch seam allowances). Cut two pieces of fabric to these measurements for the front and back. *Note:* For a center-back opening, add an extra 1¼-inch seam allowance to the width or length of the cushion back and cut the back into two equal pieces. *Ruffle:* Measure one edge of the form and multiply by four, then multiply again by two. Decide on the width of your ruffle, then double this measurement and add 1¼ inches (for ⅝-inch seam allowances). Cut and piece together bias fabric strips to the desired length.

SINGLE RUFFLE

1 Use French seams to stitch the ruffle strips into a ring. Press under the bottom edge to form a double ⅜-inch hem. Pin, baste, and stitch.

2 Mark the perimeter of the front cover and the ruffle edge in the same number of equal sections. Sew two rows of gathering stitches across each section of the ruffle.

3 Match the sections of the ruffle to the sections on the cover, pulling up the gathers to fit. Pin, baste, and stitch in place. Complete the cover as for a basic cover (see pages 14–17) or add a zipper in the back (see pages 20 and 21).

ADDING RUFFLES TO SQUARE COVERS

To make a ruffle easier to add to a square cover, gently round off the corners of your cover pieces (try drawing your curved corner around an upside-down juice glass or egg cup.)

DOUBLE RUFFLE

1 Join the ruffle strips together into a ring with plain seams, using ⅝-inch seam allowances. Trim and press the seams open. Fold the ruffle in half with wrong sides together and raw edges matching.

2 As directed for the single-ruffle cover, mark the ruffle and cover into sections, gather up the ruffle, and stitch to the front cover piece. Finish the cushion cover.

3 On square and rectangular covers, allow extra gathers around the corners. Then, when the cover is turned right side out, the ruffle will look full at each corner and not strained.

Braids and cords

Braids and cords offer yet another look. Flat braids are easier to apply before making up your cover, while chunky cords can be hand-sewn around the outside edge of a finished cover. In the latter instance, it sometimes is easier if the cover has its form added first so the outer edge is more prominent. Then the finished result is readily apparent as the cord is stitched into place. Flanged cords and braids—those attached to a flat tape—can be added in the same way as a covered piping cord (see pages 32 and 33).

MATERIALS: *Braid-trimmed cushion, 14×18 inches:* ½ yard of 45-inch-wide furnishing fabric, 1¾ yards of 1-inch-wide decorative braid, 14×18 inch cushion form, matching thread, tape measure, scissors, pins, needles
Cord-trimmed cushion, 16×16 inches: ½ yard of 45-inch-wide furnishing fabric, 2¼ yards of chunky cord, 16×16-inch cushion form, matching thread, tape measure, scissors, pins, needles

FABRIC: *Braid-trimmed cushion, front:* Measure the width and length of the form and add an extra 1¼ inches to both measurements (for ⅝-inch seam allowances). Cut one rectangle of fabric to this size. *Back:* Cut another rectangle of fabric the same size as the front, but add an additional 1¼ inches to the width or the length for a center-back opening. Cut the back into two equal pieces.
Cord-trimmed cushion, front: Measure the width and length of the form and add 1¼ inches to both measurements (for ⅝-inch seam allowances). Cut one square of fabric to this size. *Back:* Cut one piece of fabric to the same size as the front, but add an additional 1¼ inches to the width or length for the center-back opening. Cut the back into two equal pieces.

BRAID-TRIMMED CUSHION

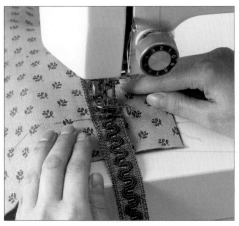

1 Mark a guideline for the braid on the right side of the front cushion piece, using basting stitches 1¾ inches in from the outer edge (this will ensure the braid is clearly displayed on the cushion). Beginning at the center of the bottom edge, lay the braid right side up with the outer edge even with the marked line; pin and baste in place. Stitch along the outer edge of the braid only, up to the first corner.

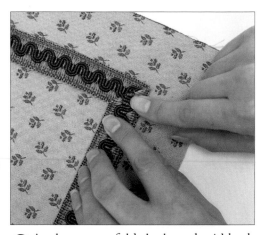

2 At the corner, fold the loose braid back down over the stitched braid, then fold the loose braid diagonally at the corner, forming a right angle. Press the fold firmly (to create a guide for stitching).

3 Lift the braid up and stitch along the pressed diagonal line. Then fold the braid back into position and stitch along the outer edge of the braid to the next corner, making sure the stitching and the braid are in a straight line. Repeat the process on all remaining corners and edges. Fasten the thread ends on the wrong side of the fabric.

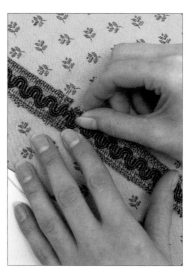

4 Join the trimmed ends of the braid together, centering them at the bottom edge. Complete by stitching along the inner edge of the braid. Add a fastening to the center-back seam, then finish stitching the cushion, as desired.

CORD-TRIMMED CUSHION

1 For this type of trim, simply hand-sew a chunky cord around the outer edge of a cover. Stitch the cover with a center-back opening. Then, beginning in the center of the bottom edge, lay the cord along the seam line. Hand-sew the cord to the seam line. At each corner, tie a knot in the cord before stitching along the next edge.

2 At the center on the bottom edge of the cushion cover, carefully snip one stitch in the seam to form a small gap. Unravel the cord ends. Cross over the cord ends and push into the gap. Sew the seam closed, neatly enclosing the ends of the cord.

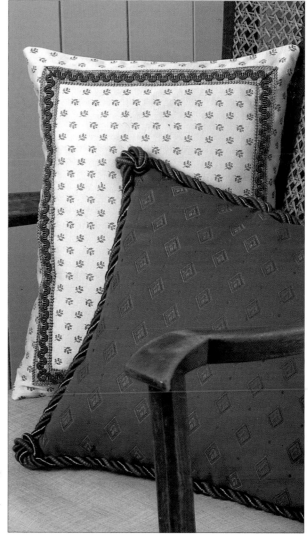

Fabric tassels

For this distinctive trim idea, create tassels from fabric and tack them to the four corners of your cushion. Here, they're added to a basic cushion made up with a simple slip-stitched opening along one edge. Stitch the tassels and cushion in matching fabrics as shown here. Or, use a mix of contrasting materials and play with the arrangement of the tassels.

MATERIALS: *Square cover, 16×16 inches, with 8-inch-long tassels:* 1½ yards of 55-inch-wide furnishing fabric, large sheet of graph paper, 16×16-inch cushion form, matching thread, small amount of fiberfill, pearl cotton thread, tape measure, scissors, pins, needles

FABRIC: *Front and back:* Measure the width and length of the form and add 1¼ inches to both measurements (for ⅝-inch seam allowances). Cut two squares of fabric to this size. *Tassels:* Draw up the pattern for the tassel as shown in Step 1 below and cut out eight shapes from the fabric.

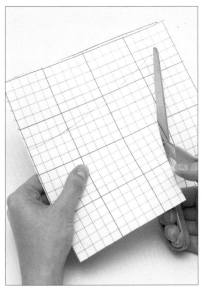

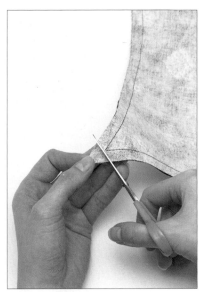

1 Make the cushion cover following instructions for basic square cover (see pages 14 and 15). For tassels, cut a 16×16-inch square from graph paper. Fold paper into quarters. Draw the pattern onto paper as shown here. Cut out pattern and unfold. Then cut out eight pieces of fabric to this pattern.

2 For each tassel, place two fabric pieces together with right sides facing. Pin, baste, and stitch together, using a ⅜-inch seam allowance and leaving an opening for turning the shape right side out. Trim the corners and turn the shape right side out. Slip-stitch the opening closed.

3 Thread a needle with a double sewing thread and knot the end. Baste a 2×2-inch square in the center on the wrong side of the tassel using the thread; stitch through both layers, taking a small stitch at each corner before moving the thread to the next corner. Do not cut the thread. Place a small ball of fiberfill in the center of the marked square.

4 Pull up the stitches to enclose the fiberfill and form the head of the tassel. Round off the head, adjusting gathers as necessary, and knot the thread. To secure the tassel, thread a needle with a length of pearl cotton and wind it around, just beneath the fiberfill head, about five or six times. Fasten off and thread the end inside the bound threads.

5 Hand-sew the tassel to a corner of the cushion cover, stitching through the top of the tassel head.

6 Make three more tassels in the same manner and add to your cover.

Piping

Piping is a strip of bias fabric that is folded in half and inserted into a seam. Cord can be added inside the folded fabric, giving it a harder edge. Piping cord comes in a variety of thicknesses, ranging from ¼ inch to ¾ inch in diameter. Select piping to suit the style of your cushions by wrapping the piping fabric around different thicknesses of cord until you get the result you want. Create added flair by ruching the covering fabric. To do this, cut bias strips in the usual manner, but allow two to three times the length of the piping cord. With piped designs, place the cushion opening in the middle of one edge, behind the cord, or across the back of the cushion. Gently round off the corners as for ruffled cushions, if desired (see page 27).

MATERIALS: *Piped cushion, 15×15 inches:* ¾ yard of 55-inch-wide furnishing fabric, 15×15-inch square cushion form, piping cord, matching thread, tape measure, scissors, pins, needles

FABRIC: *Front and back:* Measure the width and length of the form and add 1¼ inches to both measurements (for ⅝-inch seam allowances). Cut two pieces of fabric to this size. *Note:* For a center-back opening, add an extra 1¼ inches to the width or length of the cushion back and cut the back into two equal pieces. *Piping:* Measure the length of one side of the cushion form and multiply by four, then add an extra 4 inches for joining. For the width, measure around the piping cord and add 1¼ inches (for ⅝-inch seam allowances). Cut and piece bias fabric strips to the desired length.

1 Cut out the bias strips. Pin, baste, and stitch the strips together into one long length, using ¼-inch seam allowances. Fold the bias strip evenly in half around a length of piping cord. Using a piping foot, machine-stitch along the cord to hold it in place.

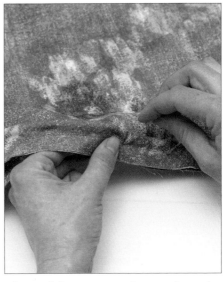

2 On a square cover, position the piping around all four sides of the front cushion piece, matching the raw edges of piping with the raw edges of the cover, as shown. At each corner, snip into the piping fabric up to the stitching to help form sharp corners.

3 On round covers, clip into the piping seam allowance at regular intervals, making clips about 1 inch apart, to help ease piping around cover.

4 Pin, baste, and stitch the piping in place, ending the stitching 2 inches before the join. Trim the piping so that it overlaps the opposite end by 1 inch. Unpick 1 inch of the stitching from each end of the piping. Trim the cord so that the ends butt together exactly. Turn under the last ⅝ inch of the piping strip and overlap the opposite end. Pin, baste, and finish stitching the piping into position.

5 Make up the cushion back with a center closure. Place the cushion front and back together with right sides facing. Pin, baste, and machine-stitch all around the cover, close to the piping, using a zipper foot. Trim and turn right side out. Press so the piping is right at the edge. Insert form. Sew the opening closed.

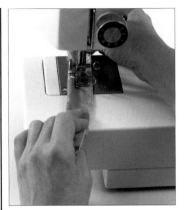

GATHERED PIPING

1 Place the cord inside the bias strip in the same way as for corded piping. Stitch across the end of the folded strip, catching the end of the cord. Pin, baste, and stitch along the cord, but not tight up against it, for approximately 8 inches.

2 Leaving the needle in the fabric, raise the machine foot. Gently pull cord through fabric to gather the covering. Repeat along entire length of cord. Attach piping to cover, trimming off the holding stitches and joining the ends together as directed in steps 2–4. Make sure fabric is evenly gathered over the join. Assemble the cushion.

Ties and buttons

Ties always make attractive fasteners, while buttons look smart with envelope-style covers. In our tied example, straight fabric ties are knotted together at one side of the cover. When the form is added, the inside flap is clearly visible so an attractive contrasting fabric will accentuate the detail. The buttoned cover uses a contrasting half-lining to make a border and to provide extra support for the buttons and buttonholes without affecting the sharp bottom corners. Cover the buttons with the lining fabric.

MATERIALS: *Cushion with flap and ties, 14×14 inches:* ½ yard of 45-inch-wide striped fabric, ¼ yard of 36-inch-wide gingham fabric for flap and ties, 14×14-inch cushion form, matching thread, tape measure, scissors, pins, needles

Envelope-style cushion cover with buttons and buttonholes, 14×14 inches: ¾ yard of 55-inch-wide furnishing fabric, ½ yard of 45-inch-wide furnishing fabric for lining, 14×14-inch cushion form, matching thread, three ¾-inch-diameter self-covering buttons, tape measure, scissors, pins, needles

FABRIC: *Cushion with flap and ties, front and back:* Measure the width and length of the form and add 1¼ inches to both measurements (for ⅝-inch seam allowances). Cut out two squares of fabric to this size. *Flap:* Cut a piece of fabric to the same width as the back and 6¼ inches deep. *Ties:* Cut four 3½×10-inch strips of fabric.

Envelope-style cushion cover with buttons and buttonholes, front and back: Measure the form widthwise and add 1¼ inches (for ⅝-inch seam allowances). Measure the length of the form and add 5¼ inches for turn-down flap and seam allowance. Cut two pieces of main fabric to these measurements for front and back. *Lining:* Cut two pieces of lining fabric to the same width as the cover, only 10 inches long.

TIES

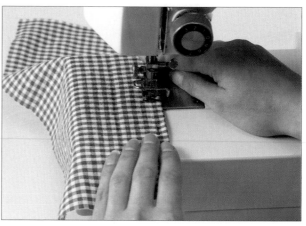

1 Fold one tie piece in half lengthwise with right sides facing. Pin, baste, and stitch the long side and one short side together, using ⅜ inch for the seam allowance. Trim and turn the tie right side out. Stitch three more ties in the same manner.

2 Turn under a double ⅜-inch hem on the long bottom edge of the flap. Pin, baste, and stitch the hem.

3 Place the raw edges of two ties on the right side edge of the cushion front, 3¼ inches in from each side; pin, baste, and stitch. Fold over a double ⅜-inch hem along this edge, including the ends of the ties. Pin, baste, and stitch the hem.

4 Pin the two remaining ties with their raw edges to the right side edge of the cushion back, matching the front ties. Now place cover pieces with right sides together, keeping the front hemmed edge ¾ inch below top edge of back. Place the right side of the flap over the cushion front, matching the sides and the top raw edge with the back. Pin, baste, and stitch around the cover, avoiding the ties. Trim and turn cover right side out. Insert form, pushing the flap over it. Knot ties together.

ENVELOPE COVER WITH BUTTONS

1 Place the front and back cushion pieces with right sides facing and the raw edges matching. Pin, baste, and stitch the long sides and the short bottom edge. Place lining pieces with right sides facing and the raw edges matching; pin, baste, and stitch the short sides. Turn under a double ⅜-inch hem along the bottom edge of the lining; pin, baste, and stitch hem.

2 Place the lining and fabric covers with right sides facing and seams matching. Pin, baste, and stitch together around the top edge. Trim and turn the lining up and then press. Push the lining down inside the main cover, leaving a ⅜-inch band of lining showing around the top edge. Pin, baste, and stitch all around the top edge, following the first seam line.

3 Fold over the open edge 4¾ inches. Mark positions for three buttonholes, 3½ inches in from the side edges and 3½ inches apart. Machine-stitch a buttonhole at each marked position through both flap sections. Stitch a corresponding button (see page 19, Covering Buttons) to the front cover at each marked position. Insert your form and fasten the buttons closed.

Creative Cushions

Use cushions in a creative way to echo aspects of your personality and the room's design. You'll be amazed at how easily your decor can be transformed. Choose an interesting shape, an unusual fabric, a fun trim, or buttons to make your cushion unique. Then push your imagination even further. Try making covers from household towels, place mats, and fashionable scarves. Experiment by cutting and stitching scraps together to form patchwork patterns or by pleating and tucking the material to create different shapes. Or, fill them with plastic-foam beads to create bean bags children are sure to enjoy. Whatever you choose, your cushions will have that touch of individuality that store-bought equivalents can't deliver.

Quick covers

Before you embark on a costly search for fabric, look around the house for items that can be put to a new use as cushion covers. Cotton/linen dish towels, seldom-worn scarves, napkins, and place mats easily stitch up into attractive cushion covers. This approach allows minimal expense, time, and stitching to create the maximum impact.

MATERIALS: *Laced dish-towel cover, 14×14 inches:* One dish towel approximately 28×20½ inches, eyelet kit for ½-inch-diameter eyelets, 14×14-inch cushion form, 1⅓ yards each of ¾-inch-wide ribbon in two different colors; tape measure, scissors, pins, needles
Napkin cover, about 15×15 inches: Two square napkins approximately 19×19 inches, matching thread, 15x15-inch cushion form, yarn and bodkin for making pom-pom, tape measure, scissors, pins, needles

LACED DISH-TOWEL COVER

1 Press under 3¼ inches at the long edges of dish towel. Mark and fix eyelets along each short edge, placing eyelets in pairs spaced 1 inch apart. Affix top and bottom eyelet pairs through both layers of the pressed edge, starting 1 inch in from the top and bottom edges. Center second eyelet pair in between, affixing the eyelets through just one towel layer.

2 Place the cushion form centered on the wrong side of the towel, tucking it under the long edges. Take the first length of ribbon and, working from the bottom edge, lace the short bottom edges together up to the center as you would a shoe. Tie into a knot and then into a bow. Repeat with a second ribbon, lacing from the top edge to the center.

MAKING A POM-POM

Pom-poms make an attractive addition to all kinds of cushions. From cardboard, cut two 2-inch-diameter circles with a ⅜-inch-diameter hole in the center. Place the rings together. Using a bodkin, wind wool yarn around them until the hole is filled. Snip through the yarn strands around the outer edge of the rings. Then gently ease the two rings apart and secure the pom-pom by threading and knotting a strand of yarn around the center. Remove rings.

NAPKIN COVER

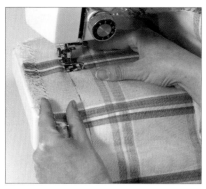

1 Pin and baste two napkins together with wrong sides facing. Topstitch all around, 1½ inches from the outer edge, leaving a center opening in one side. Work a second line of stitching ¼ inch in from the first line. Insert form. Close the opening by completing the two rows of topstitching.

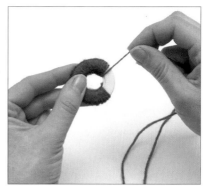

2 Make a 1½-inch-diameter pom-pom (see Making a Pom-Pom, page 38). Take the long end of the yarn from the center of the pom-pom, thread it through a needle, then push the threaded needle through the middle of the cushion. Push it back through the cushion again from the other side, pulling the center of the form together. Stitch through pom-pom base to secure.

OTHER QUICK IDEAS
Gathered dish-towel cover

Fold a dish towel in half with right sides facing. Stitch the two side seams, leaving the top edge open. Turn right side out and insert form. Gather opening and hold it in place with a rubber band. Tie and knot a piece of ribbon over the rubber band and sew a small bell to each end of the ribbon.

Scarf bolster

Spread out a scarf with the wrong side up. Place a piece of high-loft batting, narrower than the scarf, in the center and roll the scarf up tightly to form a bolster shape. Secure the gathered scarf ends with rubber bands, then cover them with ribbon ties.

Kids' cushions

Cushions aren't just for decoration and comfort—they also can provide hours of fun for younger members of the family. Cube-shape cushions filled with ultralight plastic-foam beads serve as building blocks, while ball-shape cushions are perfect for rolling all around the house.

MATERIALS: *Cube-shape cushion, approximately 12×12 inches:* ⅞ yard of 55-inch-wide furnishing fabric, plastic-foam beads for filler, matching thread, tape measure, scissors, pins, needles
Ball-shape cushion, approximately 12½ inches in diameter: Paper for pattern, ¾ yard of 45-inch-wide furnishing fabric, plastic-foam beads for filler, matching thread, tape measure, scissors, pins, needles

FABRIC: *Cube-shape cushion:* If your fabric has a strong decorative motif, you might want to alter the cushion size (or the amount of fabric) so the motif can be positioned in the center of each of the six sides of the cube.
Ball-shape cushion: Enlarge the pattern, page 91, for one cushion section onto paper, using a grid of 1 square = ¾ inch. Cut out six pattern pieces, placing the pattern on the straight grain of the fabric and adding a ⅜-inch seam allowance all around.

CUBE-SHAPE CUSHION

1 Spread out the fabric and carefully mark a 12×12-inch square (placing any strong motif in the center). Add a ⅝-inch seam allowance. Use this square as the pattern for cutting out five more squares.

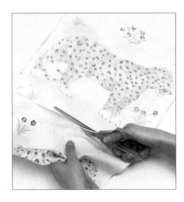

2 Place four squares in a row. With right sides facing and raw edges matching, pin, baste, and stitch sides of squares together, forming a ring; start and stop stitching ⅝ inch from top and bottom edge.

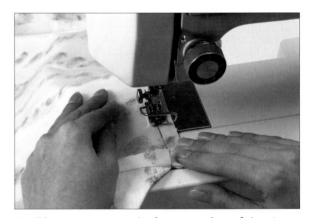

3 Place a square at the bottom edge of the ring, matching corners to seams. Pin, baste, and stitch in place, pivoting the needle at each corner. The side seams will fan out, helping to form sharp corners. Stitch top square in place in the same way, leaving a center opening in one side. Trim seams, turn cube right side out, and press. Fill with plastic-foam beads to form cube. Turn in the edges along the opening and hand-sew closed. Use tiny slip-stitches so the beads can't escape.

BALL-SHAPE CUSHION

1 Place two sections together with right sides facing. Pin, baste, and stitch together along one edge. Pin, baste, and stitch a third piece to one side. You now have half the ball. Repeat, to form the second half of the ball.

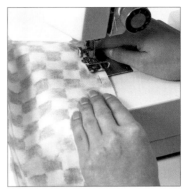

2 Pin the halves together with right sides facing. Baste and stitch together, leaving a center opening in one seam for turning right side out.

3 Trim seams and turn the ball right side out. Carefully fill with plastic-foam beads. Turn under edges on the opening and slip-stitch closed.

FILLING YOUR CUSHION

When filling a shape with plastic-foam beads, use a large household funnel or make a cone from an empty cereal box and pour your beads through it. This should help prevent beads from escaping to the floor.

Pencil cushion

Don't write off interesting and unusual shapes when designing your cushions. People of all ages enjoy cushions with a note of humor. For example, a single pencil shape is easy to stitch into a long pillow, while three pencils in a row make a fun chair cushion. Colorful felt is a good material to choose for this style, especially if the cushions are for a child's room.

MATERIALS: *Chair back cushion (only), 12¾×15½ inches:* ¾ yard of blue felt, one 6×20-inch piece each of orange and green felt, one 6×6-inch piece of navy felt, one 6½×10½-inch piece of beige felt, chalk pencil, matching threads, ¾ yard each of ⅛-inch-wide blue, orange, and green ribbon, plastic-foam beads for filler, tape measure, scissors, pins, needles

FABRIC: *Front:* Enlarge patterns for pencil body, top, lead, and base, page 90, so 1 square = ¾ inch. Cut out three bodies and three leads from orange, blue, and green felt, three pencil tops from beige felt, and three pencil bases from navy felt. Mark lines down each pencil body piece with chalk pencil. *Note:* A ¼-inch seam allowance and/or overlap is included in pattern pieces. *Back:* Use completed cushion front as a template for the back. Cut the back from blue felt.

1 Pin ribbon down each marked line on the pencil bodies. Zigzag-stitch over the ribbon. Use blue ribbon on the orange body, orange ribbon on the green body, and green ribbon on the blue body.

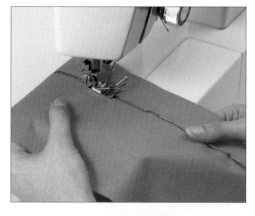

2 For each pencil, put the base piece in position, overlapping the bottom of the pencil body ¼ inch. Satin-stitch (a close zigzag stitch) in place. Add the pencil top and lead in the same manner. Repeat for each pencil.

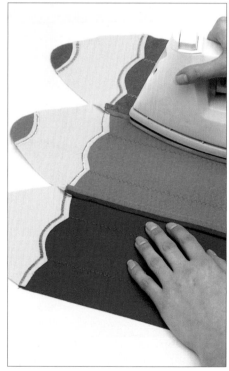

3 With right sides facing and ¼-inch seams, pin, baste, and stitch pencils in a row. Press seams open.

4 Use the completed front as a pattern and cut out one complete back section from blue felt. Pin, baste, and stitch back to front with right sides facing and leaving the base edge open.

5 Trim and turn right side out. Turn under the bottom edge ¼ inch and pin. To shape the pencils, topstitch along the existing seam lines between the pencils. Fill each pencil with the plastic-foam beads and slip-stitch the bottom edge closed.

Patchwork covers

Patchwork is a classic and enduring style because it's fun to do and ideal for using up all those leftover pieces of fabric. You can use a variety of fabric types to create any one of these designs, but it's best to mix materials of similar weights whenever possible for ease in construction and to achieve the most satisfactory results.

MATERIALS: *Crazy patchwork cushion, 16×16 inches:* Assorted scraps of fabrics, such as narrow-wale corduroy, cotton velveteen, and brocade in rich colors, ½ yard of muslin for patchwork foundation, ⅓ yard of fabric for cushion back, matching thread, pearl cotton thread in a contrasting color, embroidery needle, 16×16-inch cushion form, tape measure, scissors, pins, needles
Seminole patchwork cushion, 16×16 inches: ¼ yard each of four different 36-inch-wide cotton fabrics, ½ yard of cotton fabric for cushion back, 16×16-inch cushion form, thread to match main fabric, tape measure, scissors, pins, needles
Cathedral window patchwork cushion, 12×16 inches: 1 yard of muslin, 6×8-inch rectangles of four different silk fabrics for centers, ⅓ yard of backing fabric, matching threads, sequins, cushion form, tape measure, scissors, pins, needles

FABRIC: *Crazy patchwork cover, front:* Cut one 17×17-inch square of muslin. *Back:* Cut two 9×17-inch pieces of fabric for the back. *Patches:* Cut patches in various shapes and sizes from fabrics such as corduroy, velveteen, and brocade.
Seminole patchwork cover, front: The front consists of 2×2-inch squares stitched from strips of 2½-inch-wide fabric. *Back:* Two 9×17-inch pieces of cotton.
Cathedral window patchwork cover, front: The front consists of 12 muslin squares, each measuring 8½×8½ inches. The 17 inset squares are 2½×2½ inches. *Back:* Cut two 9×13-inch pieces of backing fabric.

CRAZY PATCHWORK

1 Allowing a ½-inch seam allowance all around the muslin square, lay patches over the muslin and rearrange to your satisfaction. Pin in position.

2 On overlapping edges of the patches, turn under ¼ inch. (Start with the patch closest to the muslin.) Pin, then baste in place.

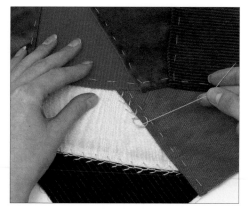

3 Using pearl cotton thread, embroider feather stitches around the edges of your patches. Stitch up the cushion back with a center opening (see pages 20 and 21), then finish the cushion as desired.

SEMINOLE PATCHWORK

1 Cut three 2½×20-inch strips from each of four cotton fabrics. Using ¼-inch seam allowances, stitch strips together, then cut eight 2½-inch-wide strips across seams.

2 Stitch four strips together in checkerboard fashion, moving strips down one square as you add each strip. Repeat twice with remaining strips. Join sections.

3 Press pieced fabric on reverse side. Cut out front. Stitch back with a center opening, using a ¼-inch seam allowance (see pages 20 and 21). Finish cushion.

CATHEDRAL WINDOW PATCHWORK

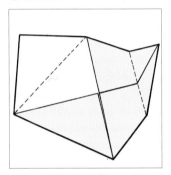

1 For each square, press under ¼ inch on all edges. Fold the square in quarters to establish the center. Lay the square wrong side up and press each corner diagonally to the center. The square should measure 5½×5½ inches. Press the corners diagonally to the center again. The square now measures 4×4 inches. Tack the four center points to hold.

2 Make up the cushion front by stitching the squares together into a rectangle. Place the first two squares with folded sides facing and overcast the edges. Open out flat and press.

3 Cut 2½-inch squares from the silk fabrics. Pin a square of silk diagonally over each overcast join. On each edge of the silk square, from the center, roll back the folded edges of the backing fabric over the raw edge of the silk, tapering off to a point at each corner. Work a double backstitch at each end, then hand-sew along the rolled back edge, through all layers. Repeat until the squares form one large rectangle. Hand-sew sequins at intersections. Stitch back with a center opening, using ½-inch seams (see pages 20 and 21). Finish cover by hand-sewing back to front.

Miters and knots

With a minimum of stitching, you can create truly smart cushion covers. Mitered covers depend on careful cutting and pattern-matching to produce their geometric effect. The triangles of fabric are seamed together to meet at the center, forming a frame. The look is especially effective if you use a fabric with strong horizontal or vertical lines. The second cushion design features knotted corners. Stitched from two pieces of fabric cut with extended corners, the cover forms a soft, pleasing outline when the corners are tied in knots.

MATERIALS: *Mitered cushion, 16×16 inches:* Paper for pattern, ⅛ yard of 55-inch-wide furnishing fabric, 16×16-inch cushion form, matching thread, large decorative bead for center of cushion, tape measure, scissors, pins, needles
Cushion with knotted corners, 16×16 inches (excluding the knotted corners): Paper for pattern, 1¾ yard of 55-inch-wide furnishing fabric, 16×16-inch cushion form, matching thread, tape measure, scissors, pins, needles

FABRIC: *Mitered cushion, front:* Draw up a pattern as shown in Step 1 and use this to cut the four front triangles. *Back:* Cut one piece to the size of the cushion form, adding 1¼ inches (for ⅝-inch seam allowances). For a center-back opening, add an additional 1¼ inches to the width (or length) and cut shape in half.
Cushion with knotted corners, front: Enlarge pattern, pages 90 and 91, for half of the cushion, using a grid of 1 square = ¾ inch. Cut one front, placing the straight edge of the pattern on the fabric fold and adding a ⅝-inch seam allowance to the remaining edges. *Back:* Cut two of the half patterns, adding a ⅝-inch seam allowance all around.

MITERED CUSHION

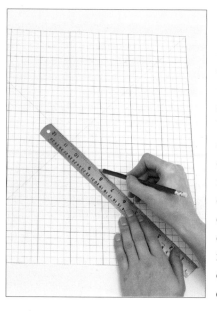

1 Measure the cushion form and draw a square to this size on a sheet of paper. Using a ruler, draw a diagonal line from one corner to the opposite corner. Repeat for other two corners. Cut out triangles.

2 Lay the triangles on your fabric so you get the same part of the fabric's pattern on each one. On striped fabric, position the triangular pieces facing up or down on the fabric. However, on a one-way design, position each triangle facing the same direction. Carefully cut out each piece, adding a ⅝-inch seam allowance all around.

3 Pin two triangles together, right sides facing and matching the pattern exactly. Baste and stitch along one short edge. Repeat with remaining two triangles. Press open.

4 Place the two sets of triangles together with right sides facing. Pin, baste, and stitch together to form the front, carefully matching the pattern across the seam.

5 Stitch two back pieces together, adding a center fastening if desired (see pages 20 and 21). Place cushion front and back pieces with right sides facing; pin, baste, and stitch together all round. Trim and turn right side out. Hand-sew bead to the center front. Insert cushion form and close the opening.

CUSHION WITH KNOTTED CORNERS

1 Place back pieces with right sides facing. Using ⅝ inch for seam allowances, pin, baste, and stitch pieces together, adding a center back opening (see pages 20 and 21). Place back and front cover pieces with right sides together and matching outer edges. Pin, baste, and stitch together all around.

2 Trim seams and turn cushion right side out. Press seams. Insert the cushion form.

3 Close the opening. Then knot each extended corner and arrange decoratively.

Pleats and tucks

Classic pleats and tucks provide an understated texture for elegant silk cushions. On the pleated cushion, the pleats are stitched in straight lines, only in different widths to add interest to an otherwise plain cover. On the tucked cushion, ³⁄₈-inch tucks are stitched into a four-sectioned cover, creating a rippled patchwork effect. The squares are seamed together with the tucks lying in different directions.

MATERIALS: *Pleated cushion, 14×14 inches:* Tissue paper for pattern, ½ yard of 55-inch-wide silk; 14×14-inch cushion form, matching thread, tape measure, scissors, pins, needles
Tucked cushion, 14×14 inches: ⅞ yard of 55-inch-wide silk, 14×14-inch cushion form, matching thread, one 1¼-inch-diameter self-cover button, tape measure, scissors, pins, needles

FABRIC: *Pleated cushion, front:* Cut a piece of fabric 15¼×31¼ inches. *Back:* Measure the cushion form width and length. Add 1¼ inches to each of the measurements (for ⅝-inch seam allowances all around). Cut one piece of fabric to these measurements.
Tucked cushion, front: The front is divided into four equal sections. Cut four 8¾×15½-inch pieces of silk. (You may want to cut a longer piece to allow for slight discrepancies in tuck measurements and stitching.) *Back:* Measure the cushion form widthwise and lengthwise and add 1¼ inches (for a ⅝-inch seam allowance). Cut one piece of fabric to this size.

PLEATED CUSHION

1 Cut a sheet of tissue paper 15¼×30 inches. Draw your pleat arrangement onto the paper. Lay out the front cushion fabric right side up. Pin the tissue paper pattern onto the fabric, with the ends ⅝ inch in from the short edges. Baste through the paper and fabric along each line. Then carefully pull away the tissue paper, leaving the basting stitches in place.

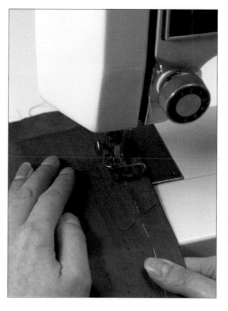

2 Form each pleat by folding the fabric with wrong sides facing and matching two lines of basting stitches. Pin, baste, and stitch. Pleat across fabric until it is 15¼×15¼ inches.

3 Press each pleat along the fold, then press all the pleats so they lie in the same direction. Baste over the seam lines all around the outer edge, securing the pleats in place.

4 Place back and front pieces with right sides facing and outer edges matching. Pin, baste, and stitch round outer edge, leaving a center opening in the bottom edge. Trim seams; turn cushion right side out. Insert cushion form. Turn in edges at opening; sew closed.

TUCKED CUSHION

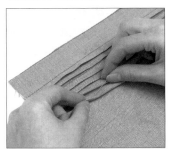

1 Beginning ⅝ inch from one short edge, fold, pin, and stitch ⅜-inch-wide tucks all across one of the four front sections, making a square. Press all the tucks in one direction. Stitch along each side to hold tucks in place. Mark a line down the center of the square across the tucks. Stitch against the direction of tucks.

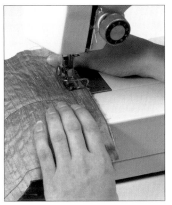

2 Stitch the remaining squares in the same manner. Then, pin two squares together with the tucks at right angles; baste and stitch the squares together. Stitch the second pair of squares together in the same manner.

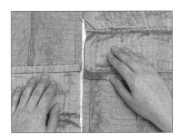

3 Place the two halves together so the tucks are at right angles. Pin, baste, and stitch the halves together to complete the cushion front.

4 Place front and back together with right sides facing. Pin, baste, and stitch all around, leaving an opening in the bottom edge. Trim and turn right side out. Cover button with fabric to match the cover (see Covering Buttons, page 19) and sew to the center of the cover. Insert cushion form and slip-stitch opening closed.

A touch of glamour

Sophisticated cushion covers are an inexpensive way to add a touch of glamour to your home. When choosing fabric for this kind of cover, walk past the furnishing and dressmaking fabrics and head straight to beautiful velvets and silks in rich colors. Not only are they pleasing to the eye, they're wonderful to the touch.

MATERIALS: *Velvet-and-silk cushion, 12×12 inches, excluding 4-inch border:* Paper for pattern, 16×16-inch square of devoré velvet, 1 yard of 45-inch-wide silk, 1½ yards of gold cording, gold thread for couching the cording in place, 12×12-inch cushion form, thread to match fabric, tape measure, scissors, pins, needles

FABRIC: *Front:* Cut two 12×12-inch center squares, one from devoré velvet and one from silk, adding ⅝ inch all around for seam allowances. (Trim leftover silk yardage to measure 22¾×45 inches.) *Back:* Cut back as for front, adding 1¼ inches to the width or length for center closure; cut into two equal pieces. *Border:* Press long edges of silk yardage to center. Place long edge of pattern on folded edge(s); cut four border sections, adding ⅝ inch for seam allowances.

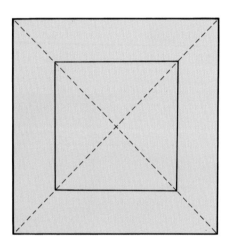

1 Measure the cushion form width and length and draw a square to this size on the paper. Draw a second square, adding 4 inches to all edges of the first square (for the border). Mark lines diagonally across the squares to ensure accurate seams at each corner. Cut out one border section and the center square; use these patterns to cut four borders, two center squares, and one back from fabrics as noted above.

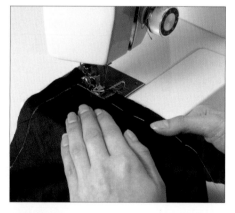

2 Open borders. With right sides facing, sew two borders together at one V-shape edge, using ⅝-inch seam allowances. Continue in this manner to form border frame. Trim, then press seams open. Refold the border and press. Baste raw edges together.

3 Lay the velvet, right side up, over the silk center square. Pin and baste together diagonally across the square in both directions and also ⅝ inch in from the outer edge. This will hold the layers in position.

4 Stitch the border frame around center square with right sides facing and raw edges even. Pin, baste, and stitch all around, following the marked seam line. Pin, baste, and stitch back sections together, adding a center fastening. Place back over front with right sides together and with the border carefully folded inside; pin, baste, and stitch together all around the outer edge. Trim, then turn cover right side out.

5 Insert cushion form and close fastening. Couch gold cording to the seam line between the center square and border. Couch the cording along each side and around the corners. Be careful not to catch the cushion form in the stitches.

Exotic cushions

Your imagination can run wild with these deliciously indulgent cushions. Let the fabrics speak for themselves. Or, add an extravagant decoration. In these examples, beaded fringe complements the brocade cushion and ruched piping gives the fun-fur cushion a soft, rounded border that is simple and stylish.

MATERIALS: *Brocade and beaded cushion, 12×16 inches:* ½ yard of 45-inch-wide brocade, 2 yards of 3-inch-wide beaded fringe trim, 2 yards of ⅝-inch-wide blue grosgrain ribbon, 2 yards of silver bead trim, matching thread, 12×16-inch cushion form, tape measure, scissors, pins, needles
Fun-fur cushion, 14×14 inches: ½ yard of 36-inch-wide fun-fur fabric, ½ yard of 45-inch-wide striped silk fabric, 1¾ yards of ¾-inch-diameter cotton cording, matching threads, 14×14-inch cushion form, tape measure, scissors, pins, needles

FABRIC: *Brocade and beaded cushion, front and back:* Measure the form length and width and add 1¼ inches to both measurements (for ⅝-inch seam allowances). Cut out two pieces of fabric to these measurements.
Fun-fur cushion, front: Measure the form in both directions and cut a piece of fur fabric to this size, adding ⅝ inch all around for seam allowances. *Back:* Cut one piece of fur fabric the same size as the front, adding an extra 1¼ inches to the width measurement for a center back seam allowance. Cut into two equal pieces.
Piping: Cut 4-inch-wide silk strips for the piping. Cut and piece piping strips together until the strip is twice the perimeter of the form.

BROCADE AND BEADS

1 Baste a line of stitches around the cushion front ⅝ inch from the raw edges. Place the ribbon to the inside of the basted outline and pin and baste in position, mitering the corners (see pages 28 and 29). Stitch the ribbon in place.

2 With right sides together, pin and baste beaded fringe to cushion front, placing the bottom edge of the fringe tape along the basted line. Join tape ends together carefully, so the lengths of the beads are evenly spaced over the join. For fullness at each corner, gather an extra 3 inches of tape and baste in place. Stitch fringe to cushion front.

3 Place cushion back to front with right sides facing. Pin, baste, and stitch all around, leaving an opening at the center bottom edge. Trim and turn right side out. Sew silver bead trim around the outer edge of the cushion, forming small loops over each corner. Insert form. Turn in edges of opening and slip-stitch the opening closed.

FUN-FUR CUSHION

1 Pin, baste, and stitch the silk strips together to the desired length. Fold the strip around the cotton cording. Pin, baste, and stitch across the end and then about 8 inches down the length. Do not stitch too close to the cord.

2 After sewing for 8 inches, leave the needle in the fabric and gently pull the cord through the fabric, creating a gathered effect. Continue in this manner until the entire length is stitched and gathered.

3 Working from the wrong side of the cushion front, baste a guideline ⅜ inch from the outer edge. With right sides facing, pin ruched piping around cushion front, raw edges matching. Join ends together at bottom edge.

4 Baste and stitch the ruched piping in place. Then stitch the back pieces together with a center opening (see pages 20 and 21). Assemble the cushion cover.

Scented cushions

Lightly scented cushions bring the sweet fragrance of summer into the house all year-round. Filled with a mixture of aromatic petals and herbs, they soothe and delight the senses when placed on a chair or scattered over a bed.

MATERIALS: *Lace-doily cushion, 9 inches in diameter, excluding ruffle:* Paper for pattern, ½ yard of 45-inch-wide cotton fabric, 4-inch-diameter lace doily, ⅞ yard of 1-inch-wide flat lace edging, 1⅔ yards of ¼-inch-wide picot-edge ribbon, matching thread, 10x19-inch piece of medium-loft batting, potpourri, 5×5-inch square of pink netting, tape measure, scissors, pins, needles *Scented rose cushion, 12×12 inches:* ½ yard of 45-inch-wide rose print fabric, 6×12-inch piece of white netting, 1⅛ yards of ¼-inch-wide ribbon, 1½ yards of 1-inch-wide white scallop trim, four ribbon roses, 12×12-inch cushion form, matching thread, potpourri, tape measure, scissors, pins, needles

FABRIC: *Lace-doily cushion, front and back:* Draw a 9-inch-diameter circle on paper for the pattern. Cut two circle patterns from fabric, adding a ⅝-inch seam allowance all around.
Scented rose cushion, front and back: Measure the cushion form lengthwise and widthwise and add 1¼ inches to both measurements (for ⅝-inch seam allowances). Cut two pieces of fabric to these measurements for the cushion front and back.

LACE-DOILY CUSHION

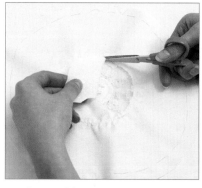

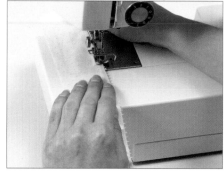

1 Pin and baste the lace doily to the center front cover piece. Machine-stitch all around the doily, close to the edge. Then zigzag-stitch over the same line. Trim away fabric from behind the lacy sections. Zigzag-stitch around the cut edges, working from the wrong side.

2 With the wrong side of the lace edging facing the right side of the cushion front and with the raw edges matching, pin and baste the lace edging around the cushion front.

3 For the ruffle, cut enough 2½-inch-wide fabric strips to measure twice the circle's circumference. Stitch strips into a ring with French seams. On one long edge, press a scant ¼-inch hem to the right side. Pin ribbon against the outside edge, covering raw edges of fabric. Stitch down both sides of the ribbon.

4 Sew gathering stitches around raw edge of ruffle; pull up gathers to fit cushion front. Pin ruffle around cushion front with right sides facing; adjust gathers. With right sides of back and front cushions facing (the ruffle in between), pin, baste, and stitch together, leaving an opening along the edge.

5 Using the paper pattern, cut two circles of batting. Center pink netting on top of one circle; baste around outer edges of netting. Place batting pieces together, netting on top. Add a bit of potpourri between the layers. Slide batting into cushion with the netting beneath the doily. Sew opening closed.

SCENTED ROSE CUSHION

1 Lay cushion front right side up. Cut two 6×6-inch squares of netting. Place one netting square atop the other; pin to the center of the cushion front. Cut ribbon into four equal lengths. Pin two ribbons to the sides, centering each ribbon along a netting edge. Baste and sew only along netting edge.

2 Add last two ribbons to the top and bottom of the netting, placing a bit of potpourri under the netting before stitching the last ribbon in place. Trim ribbon ends into inverted Vs.

3 With the right sides facing, pin and baste the scallop trim to the cushion front around the outer edge. Place front and back together with the right sides facing. Pin, baste, and stitch, leaving an opening on one side. Trim any fraying edges with pinking shears and turn right side out.

4 Hand-sew a rose to ribbon intersections. Insert the cushion form. Turn in the edges at the opening and slip-stitch the opening closed.

Floor and Seating Cushions

Besides making cushions to scatter over your chairs and sofas, consider these comfortable and attractive seating ideas. The selection of indoor cushions includes a jumbo floor cushion and a padded seat cushion for dressing up a set of kitchen chairs. To make the most of lazing around outdoors, choose the stylish foam seat suitable for a wooden bench or an easy-care cushion support to outfit your favorite summer deck chair.

Floor cushion

Floor cushions are always handy for informal, additional seating. This enormous wedge-shape is filled with soft plastic-foam beads and designed with ties—a baker's dozen in all—that allow you to join more than one cushion into any configuration you need. Tie four or more wedges together into a large square or rectangle and they become an overnight bed. Use one, or a pair, when you're short on seating space.

MATERIALS: *Floor cushion, 34¾×34¾×14¾ inches:* 2¾ yards of 60-inch-wide cotton furnishing fabric, 4½ yards of ⅜-inch-wide tape for ties, plastic-foam beads for filler, matching thread, tape measure, scissors, pins, needles

FABRIC (for one cushion): *Top:* Cut one square to measure 36×36 inches for the top. *Bottom:* Cut one 31½×36-inch rectangle for the bottom. *Back:* Cut one 16×36-inch strip for the back edge. *Sides:* Referring to the photograph, cut two triangles with the top diagonal edge measuring 36 inches, the back edge measuring 16 inches, and the bottom edge measuring 31½ inches.

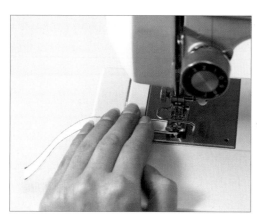

1 Cut thirteen 12-inch lengths of tape. To make each tie, fold one length in half crosswise to form a 6-inch length. Topstitch all around.

2 Pin the ties in place on each piece, matching raw ends to fabric edges. As shown, sew three ties each along the front and back of the top piece (two ties ⅝ inch in from each outer edge, one in the center). Sew one tie centered on each side of the top piece. Add ties to bottom piece in same way, omitting ties on front edge.

3 Stitch with right sides facing and use a ⅝-inch seam allowance. Pin, baste, and stitch the top to the bottom and to the back (forming a ring), starting and stopping ⅝ inch from each edge and leaving an opening in the back bottom seam.

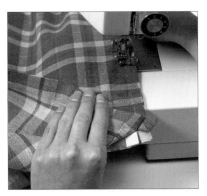

4 Pin, baste, and stitch the sides in place; the seams will split open at the ends to form neat corners. Trim seams and turn right side out.

5 Fill generously with beads and close opening with very small hand stitches or by machine-stitching across the opening.

Chair pad

Most kitchen chairs benefit from the addition of a padded cushion. The removable design is a practical choice because it's easy to launder. The decorative element is supplied by the ties that anchor the cushion to the chair. Try matching or contrasting ties made from leftover fabric, elaborate ribbon ties that criss-cross down the chair leg, or large fabric bows. For a more subtle look, fix decorative press studs or loops and toggle fastenings. A deeper pad can be made by adding a narrow 1½-inch-wide gusset between the two cushion pieces.

MATERIALS: Paper for pattern, approximately ½ yard of 45-inch-wide furnishing fabric, piping cord, approximately ⅓ yard of 36-inch-wide contrasting fabric for covering piping and toggle strips, two toggle buttons, 20 inches of ¼-inch-wide elastic, matching thread, batting for filler, tape measure, scissors, pins, needles

FABRIC: *Front and back:* Use a paper pattern to cut two pieces from your fabric, adding ⅝-inch all around for seam allowances. *Ties:* For two toggle-loops, cut two ¾×5½-inch strips of fabric. For two plain loops, cut two ¾×8-inch strips of fabric. *Piping:* Measure around the edge of the pattern and stitch covered piping to this length plus 1½ inches (see pages 32 and 33 for making piping and joining).

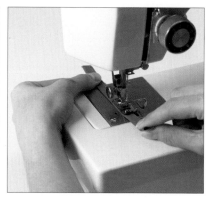

1 Lay paper over chair seat. Holding paper firmly, mark outer edge of seat, curving around chair back at back corners. Cut out pattern, snipping in around back struts for a good fit. Mark placement for two plain loops (one at each corner on the back edge) and two toggle loops (one at each back corner on sides).

2 Using the pattern, cut two fabric pieces and mark loop positions with pins. Add a line of stitching to reinforce the back corners. With the cover right side up, pin and baste piping around one cover piece to match the raw edges. Snip into the curves. Join the covered piping cord in the center of the back edge.

3 To make each toggle loop, fold fabric strip in half lengthwise. Pin, baste, and stitch down the long edge, using a ¼-inch seam allowance. Turn tube right side out. Cut a 4½-inch length of elastic and slide it inside the tube; pin at both ends to hold the elastic in place. Make two.

4 Stitch two plain loops as directed for the toggle loops, except use 5½-inch lengths of elastic. Fold each of the four loops in half; place over piping on marked positions at the back of the cushion. Pin and baste.

5 Place the second cushion piece over the first one with right sides facing and outer edges matching. Pin, baste, and stitch together, leaving an opening in the center back edge between the plain loop positions. Trim seams and turn right side out. Use the paper pattern to cut out a piece of batting. Insert the batting. Turn in the raw edges at the opening and slip-stitch closed. Hand-sew a toggle button centered on the inside of each toggle loop.

Bench seat cushion

Seat cushions for wooden benches are ideal because they can be removed easily and brought inside for a summer rain and again when winter months arrive. Choose a stylish fabric for the cover and for additional comfort, reinforce the outer edges with a rolled batting edge. A boxed cushion to fit any size seat can be made by using the same method.

MATERIALS: *Note:* You will need to determine yardage based on the size of your seat. Foam pad, 3 inches thick, the same width and length as the seat, equal amounts of furnishing fabric, lining, and batting (see below to determine yardage), hook-and-loop fastening tape 6 inches shorter than the length of the pad, matching thread and buttonhole thread, tape measure, scissors, pins, needles

FABRIC: Cut all pieces from fabric, batting, and lining. *Top and bottom:* Measure foam pad and cut two pieces to this size, adding $1\frac{3}{8}$ inches all around ($\frac{5}{8}$ inch for seam allowances, $\frac{3}{4}$ inch for padded allowances). *Back gusset:* Cut two pieces 6 inches shorter than pad length and half the depth, adding $\frac{5}{8}$-inch seam allowance all around, plus $\frac{3}{4}$ inch padded allowance to long edges. *Front/sides gusset:* Cut one strip to this size (see diagram below), adding 6 inches to complete back edge of gusset, plus $1\frac{3}{8}$ inches all around ($\frac{5}{8}$ inch for seam allowances, $\frac{3}{4}$ inch for padded allowances).

1 Place the fabric, right side facing up, atop the lining with the batting in between. Pin and baste layers together.

2 To make the back gusset opening, separate the fastening tape. Position each half over the center seam allowance of each back gusset piece; pin, baste, and stitch tape in place. Press tape together. Join front/sides gusset to each end of back gusset, making a ring.

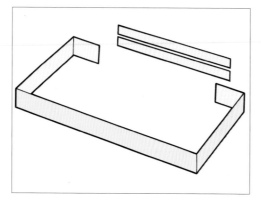

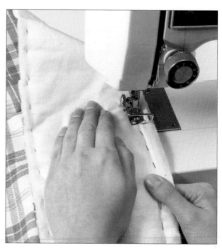

3 With right sides facing and outer edges matching, pin, baste, and stitch gusset to cushion top and bottom, placing the back opening centered across the back edge. Snip into the gusset at each corner to help form sharp corners. Turn cushion right side out.

4 Using buttonhole thread, quilt through the layers ¾ inch in from the seam line. This creates a padded, rolled edge. Continue stitching all around the top and bottom edges.

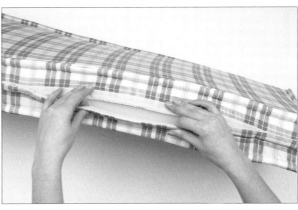

5 Insert the foam pad, fitting it neatly into the corners. Close the back opening.

Deck chair cushion

Cushions for deck or patio furniture can provide an ornamental and striking finish to traditional furniture. Size yours so they lie right across the width of your deck chair, providing the maximum comfort. Add corner eyelets so a trio can be joined together with large split curtain rings, ribbons, or tapes. The eyelets also allow you to anchor the top cushion to the top struts of the deck chair, fixing it firmly in place. Fill each cushion with washable fiberfill or make them up so the covers easily can be removed for cleaning.

MATERIALS: *One cushion, 11×16¾ inches:* ½ yard of 36-inch-wide furnishing fabric, fiberfill, eyelet kit for ⅜-inch-diameter eyelets, four 1-inch-diameter split curtain rings, sturdy rope, matching thread, tape measure, scissors, pins, needles

FABRIC: *Front:* Cut one 11×16¾-inch rectangle, adding a ⅝-inch seam allowance all around. *Back:* Cut two 8⅜×11-inch rectangles, adding a ⅝-inch seam allowance all around.

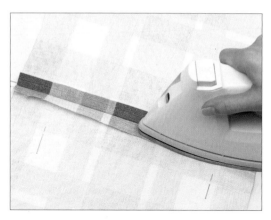

1 Place back pieces with right sides facing. Pin and stitch along one long edge, leaving a 5-inch opening in the center of the seam line. Press seam allowance open along entire length.

2 Place cushion back to cushion front with right sides facing. Pin, baste, and stitch together. Trim the seams. Turn the cover right side out through the back opening. Press cover with the seam line to the outside edge.

3 Topstitch around the cover a scant ⅛ inch from the outer edge. Then create a border (to accommodate the eyelets) by pinning and stitching a seam line 1 inch from the outer edge.

4 Mark and fix an eyelet into each corner of the cover, following the manufacturer's instructions. Insert fiberfill. Stitch opening closed.

5 To join cushions together, fix a split ring into each eyelet and link them together. Or, use lengths of tape or ribbon. Knot the upper cushion to the top struts of the deck chair using sturdy rope.

Hand-Stitched Cushions

Lovely cushions can be accented by the prettiest pieces of needlework. Most types of hand-stitching can be translated into a cushion cover. Whatever your passion—quilting, appliqué, crewel, embroidery, or needlepoint—sewing it into a cover is a practical and attractive way to showcase your skills. Just vary the cushion size to suit the method.

Quilted cushions

Several types of quilting can be used successfully for cushion covers. Two approaches are shown here—trapunto and Italian quilting. With trapunto quilting, a motif is outlined in hand-stitches and then stuffed from behind to produce raised areas. Italian quilting has evenly worked channels of stitching through which cords are pulled to form rounded furrows. When using sheer fabrics, the hues of the cord show through to the right side, adding strips of softly-shaded color.

MATERIALS: *Trapunto cushion, 12×12 inches:* ½ yard of 45-inch-wide furnishing fabric (with a prominent motif), 13×13-inch square of muslin, small amount of fiberfill, pearl cotton thread in a contrasting color, matching thread, 12×12-inch cushion form, tape measure, scissors, pins, needles
Italian-quilted cushion, 12×12 inches: ⅜ yard each of 36-inch-wide shiny, sheer fabric and solid-color poplin, bright green rug yarn, bodkin, matching thread, 12×12-inch cushion form, tape measure, scissors, pins, needles

FABRIC: *Trapunto cushion, front:* Cut one 13×13-inch square each from furnishing fabric and muslin. Make sure that the main motif is centered on the fabric piece. *Back:* Cut two 7×13-inch rectangles from the furnishing fabric.
Italian-quilted cushion, front: Cut one 13×13-inch square each from sheer fabric and poplin. *Back:* Cut two 7×13-inch rectangles from the poplin.

TRAPUNTO QUILTING

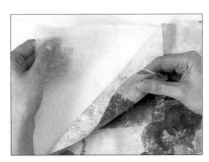

1 Pin and baste muslin to the wrong side of the fabric, matching outer edges.

2 Using pearl cotton thread and working from the right side, hand-stitch around the main motifs using small running stitches.

3 On the wrong side, gently ease (or clip) the muslin threads apart behind each stitched area and push in small amounts of fiberfill until you create a firm, rounded effect. Return the muslin threads and hold with a few hand-stitches, if necessary, to keep fiberfill in place. Prepare cushion back, using a ½-inch seam allowance. Assemble cushion as desired.

ITALIAN QUILTING

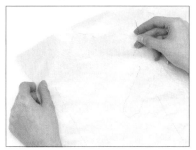 1 Baste the sheer fabric, right side up, over the solid-color poplin, working across the fabric at regular intervals to keep the sheer fabric from sliding. On paper, work out a rough sketch for the channels. Each channel will be ¼ inch wide.

 2 Using the sewing machine foot as a guide, stitch across the fabric to form a series of channels. Always work in the same direction.

 3 Thread the rug yarn onto a bodkin and thread through each channel. Leave 3-inch yarn tails hanging free at each end until all channels have been filled.

 4 To secure the ends of the channels, stitch a line around the fabric ½ inch from the edge. Trim the yarn tails to the edge of the fabric. Using a ½-inch seam allowance, stitch the cushion back with a center opening and assemble the cushion as desired.

Appliqué ideas

Appliqué—the art of applying one fabric to another—has been used to embellish clothes and furnishings in all kinds of imaginative ways for centuries. Two popular forms are felt appliqué, which uses simple, almost childlike cut-outs to great effect, and perse appliqué, where motifs from one fabric are cut out and applied to another, in effect creating a third type of fabric.

MATERIALS: *Two felt appliqué cushions, 14×14 inches and 16×16 inches:* *For both cushions:* Paper for pattern, fusible webbing, thread to match felt, tape measure, scissors, pins, needles. *For small cushion:* ½ yard of 36-inch-wide ribbed cotton fabric, 14×14-inch square of blue felt, 14×14-inch cushion form, button (optional). *For large cushion:* ⅝ yard of 36-inch-wide ribbed cotton fabric, 16×16-inch square of blue felt, 16×16-inch cushion form
Perse appliqué, 12×12 inches: ½ yard of 36-inch-wide striped fabric, 13×13-inch square of netting fabric, enough fish-motif fabric to cut out four appliqués, fusible webbing, thread to match background, small shells and starfish that can be sewn on, small beads, eight small white plastic curtain rings, 1⅔ yards of white rope, 12×12-inch cushion form, tape measure, scissors, pins, needles

FABRIC: *Felt appliqué cushions, front:* Measure the cushion form both ways and cut one piece of ribbed cotton to this size, adding a ⅝-inch seam allowance all around. *Back:* Cut back the same size as the front, adding an additional 1¼ inches to one edge. Cut into two equal pieces. *Felt decoration:* Cut one square of felt 1½ inches smaller than the finished size of the cushion front.
Perse appliqué, front: From striped fabric, cut one 13×13-inch square. *Back:* Cut two 7×13-inch rectangles of striped fabric.

FELT APPLIQUE

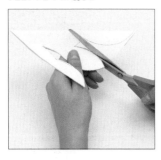

1 Cut a square of paper 1½ inches smaller than the chosen cushion size. Fold the square into quarters and then once on the diagonal, matching all folded edges. Draw your design on the triangle, remembering that the folds will produce mirror-images. Cut out pattern.

2 Iron fusible webbing onto one side of the felt. Unfold your paper pattern and use to mark the design onto the paper side of the webbing. Cut out.

3 Peel off the protective paper, center the felt design on the cushion front, and fuse in position.

4 Stitch around design outline. Pull all sewing threads to the wrong side and fasten. Stitch a cushion back with a center opening, using ½-inch seam allowances. Assemble cushion.

PERSE APPLIQUE

1 Roughly cut out four fish motifs from the fabric. Iron fusible webbing to the wrong side, then carefully cut out each fish outline.

2 Mark the center of the cushion front. Position the fish to face the center. Peel off the protective backing and fuse fish in place with an iron. Pin and baste netting over the cushion front.

3 Stitch a cushion back with a center opening, using a ½-inch seam allowance. With right sides facing, stitch cushion front to back. Trim seams and turn cover right side out. Hand-sew beads, shells, and starfish to front.

4 Hand-sew a ring at each corner and in the center of each side. Thread a length of white rope through the rings; knot ends together at one corner. Insert cushion form and close the opening.

Crewelwork cover

Crewelwork is freehand embroidery worked on fabric using embroidery wools or silks. The motifs often are taken from nature—flowers, fruits, and birds—and worked in colorful rows of filling stitches such as chain stitch, stem stitch, satin stitch, or seed stitch. By using fine stranded threads the effects are intricate and delicate, and the resulting style is a true-to-life picture.

MATERIALS: Tracing paper, pencil, two 22½×22½-inch squares of linen cloth, 12×12-inch cushion form, water-soluble marking pen, one skein each of DMC Medici wool in the colors shown on the chart (see page 74), embroidery hoop, small crewel needle, sewing needle and thread, tape measure, scissors, pins

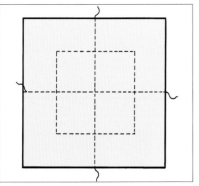

1 To prepare the fabric, measure and mark the center of one piece of linen. Baste a line vertically and horizontally across the fabric to find the center. Measure and mark a 12×12-inch square in the center of the fabric. Baste all around the square.

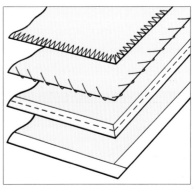

2 To prevent fraying, use any of the following: zigzag-stitch all around edges of linen by machine, overcast edges by hand, turn under edges and hem, or fold masking tape over the edges. There should be about 5 inches of border fabric around the design area.

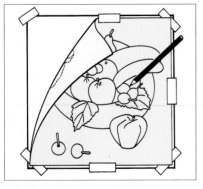

3 Transfer the full-size pattern, pages 74 and 75, onto tracing paper. To transfer the design to the fabric, tape the traced design to a bright window, then tape the fabric, centered, over the top. Use the water-soluble marking pen to trace the design onto the fabric. Remove the fabric and go over any faint sections, if necessary.

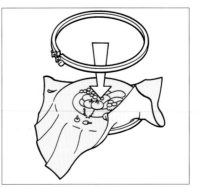

4 You will find it much easier to embroider if you fit your fabric into a special embroidery hoop. Separate the two rings by loosening the screw on the larger ring and placing the fabric centered over the smaller ring. Gently press the larger ring over the top. Now tighten the screw until the fabric is taut inside the hoop.

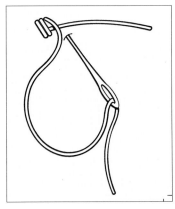

5 Following the chart and color key on pages 74 and 75, work the stitches using a double strand of wool, unless noted otherwise on the chart. For details of the stitches used, see Embroidery Stitches, pages 88 and 89. To start stitching, use a 16-inch length of thread (single or doubled) and bring it up through the fabric at the desired position. Holding the end of the thread at the back, work a few stitches over the end. For subsequent threads, run the needle under a few stitches on the wrong side. To end a length, run the needle under a few stitches on the wrong side and trim off the end.

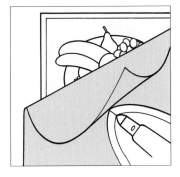

6 When the embroidery is complete, place the work face down on a soft cloth and press the back lightly with a steam iron. Let the fabric cool before moving it.

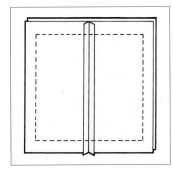

7 Stitch a cushion back, using the desired fastening method (see pages 20 and 21). With right sides facing, pin, baste, and stitch the back and front covers together to complete.

TIME-SAVING TIP

To save time, thread several needles with all the colors needed for the particular area you are embroidering. Then simply switch needles for each color.

In this example, an overlapping vent fastening was used. The border was created by hand-stitching a decorative inner seam line 2 inches in from the outer edge, following the dimensions of the cushion form.

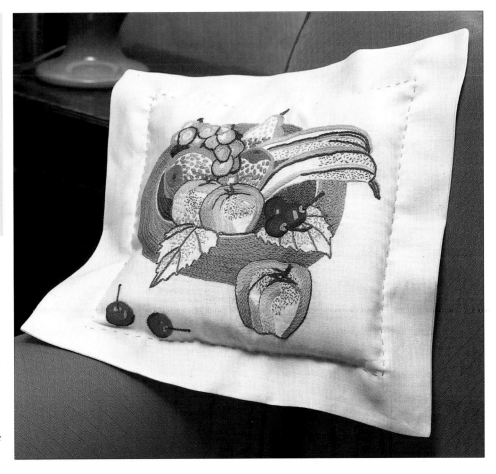

CREWELWORK COVER DESIGN AND STITCH CHART

Key to DMC Medici wools used:
pale yellow 8027
crimson 8102
red 8103
orange 8129
pale pink 8139
deep blue 8203
medium blue 8208
pale blue 8210
pale mustard 8326
pale mustard 8327
bright green 8341
deep bright green 8401
beige 8501
pale green 8567
khaki 8610
pink 8817
very pale green 8871
gray-blue 8932
deep yellow 8941
blanc white

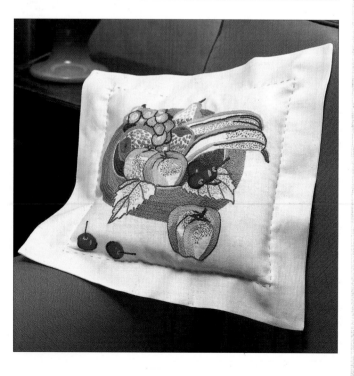

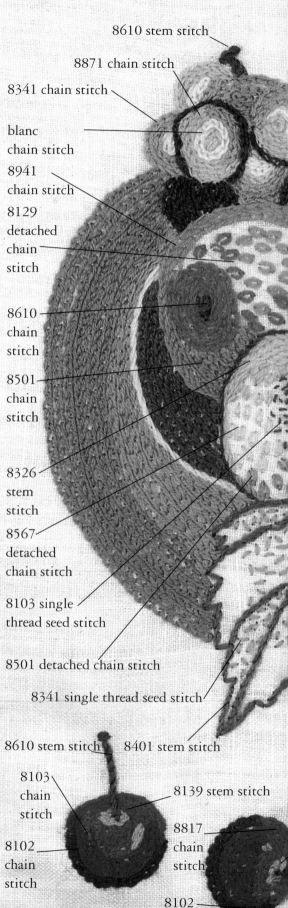

8610 stem stitch

8871 chain stitch

8341 chain stitch

blanc
chain stitch

8941
chain stitch

8129
detached
chain
stitch

8610
chain
stitch

8501
chain
stitch

8326
stem
stitch

8567
detached
chain stitch

8103 single
thread seed stitch

8501 detached chain stitch

8341 single thread seed stitch

8610 stem stitch   8401 stem stitch

8103
chain
stitch

8139 stem stitch

8817
chain
stitch

8102
chain
stitch

8102

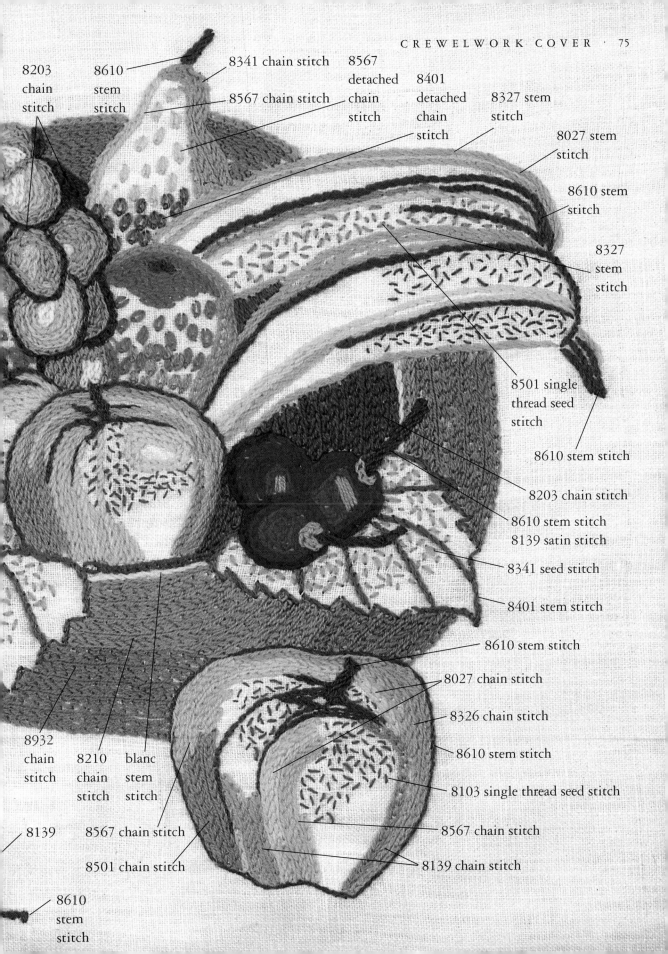

8203 chain stitch

8610 stem stitch

8341 chain stitch

8567 chain stitch

8567 detached chain stitch

8401 detached chain stitch

8327 stem stitch

8027 stem stitch

8610 stem stitch

8327 stem stitch

8501 single thread seed stitch

8610 stem stitch

8203 chain stitch

8610 stem stitch

8139 satin stitch

8341 seed stitch

8401 stem stitch

8610 stem stitch

8027 chain stitch

8326 chain stitch

8610 stem stitch

8103 single thread seed stitch

8567 chain stitch

8139 chain stitch

8932 chain stitch

8210 chain stitch

blanc stem stitch

8139

8567 chain stitch

8501 chain stitch

8610 stem stitch

Needlepoint cover

Needlepoint is a hard-wearing embroidery worked in wool over a canvas or sturdy even-weave base. Because the background is woven into even squares, each stitch is worked over one or more intersections, completely covering the background. The result is a firm fabric that is ideal for soft furnishings such as cushions and seat covers. Before you begin this needlepoint cover, identify the different yarn shades and attach a small length of each one to the appropriate color on the chart for easy reference.

MATERIALS: *Needlepoint cushion, 16×16 inches:* 20×20-inch square each of 10-mesh canvas and backing fabric, masking tape, tapestry frame, Paterna Persian yarn in the colors and amounts shown on chart (see pages 78 and 79), tapestry needle, 16×16-inch cushion form, sewing thread to match backing fabric, tape measure, scissors, pins
For blocking the piece: Blotting paper, a clean, soft board, rust-proof pins

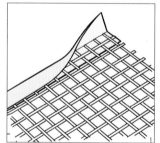

1 To prevent fraying of canvas edges, fold masking tape over them, leaving a border of about 2 inches around the design. Using yarn in a contrasting color, baste across the center of the canvas both ways to find the center. These basting stitches also can serve as stitching guidelines. Baste additional stitching guidelines at 10-hole intervals, if desired.

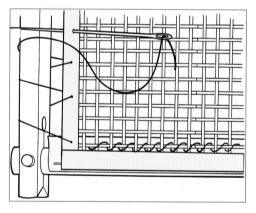

2 For ease in working the piece, fit the canvas into a tapestry frame as follows. Mark the center of the frame's webbing strips. Match these to the center of the canvas and overcast the top and bottom edges of the canvas to the webbing strips. Wind any surplus canvas around rollers until the canvas is taut. Lace side edges of canvas around side laths of frame.

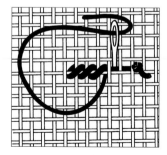

3 The wool is made up of three strands—use all of them in your needle. Work with an 18-inch length of wool. To begin, knot the end of the yarn and take it through the canvas from front to back, about 3 inches in front of the starting point. Bring the needle up at the first stitch and work the first few stitches over the end of the wool to fasten it neatly in place on the reverse side. When you reach the knot, snip it off. Start any subsequent lengths by sliding the needle under a few stitches on the reverse side. To end a length, slide the needle under a few stitches on the reverse side and trim closely.

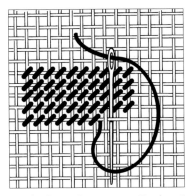

4 Work the design in half cross-stitch (see Embroidery Stitches, pages 88 and 89). Each square of the chart represents one half cross-stitch worked on the canvas. Each stitch is worked over one canvas thread intersection. All of the stitches should slope in the same direction. Make each stitch in two movements: up through the canvas and then back down. Keep one hand below the canvas to guide the needle and the other hand above it to feed the needle into the holes.

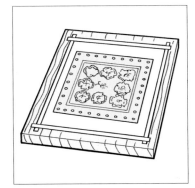

5 When the design is complete, it may need blocking to return the canvas to its original shape. On a sheet of blotting paper, mark out the original shape of the tapestry. Cover a clean, soft board with the blotting paper. Gently wet the back of the canvas with a fine spray of water. Place the canvas face down on the board and, using rust-proof pins, pin the work down, spacing the pins approximately 1 inch apart. Pull the canvas gently into shape, adjusting the pins until you are satisfied that it is correct. Let dry at room temperature and away from direct sunlight.

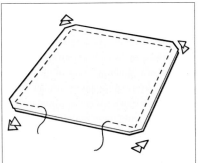

6 Cut out the canvas piece, leaving 1 inch of unworked canvas all around. Using this as a guide, cut out a piece of backing fabric to the same size. Place fabric to canvas with right sides facing. Pin, baste, and stitch all around, leaving a center opening in the bottom edge. Trim seams and turn right side out. Insert cushion form and slip-stitch the opening closed.

Key to Paterna Persian yarns used:

- 6 skeins of dark hyacinth blue 340
- 4 skeins of medium hyacinth blue 342
- 3 skeins of dark blue 540
- 2 skeins of royal blue 542
- 1 skein of light blue 545
- 2 skeins of navy blue 571
- 9 skeins of cream 764
- 2 skeins of pale orange 770
- 2 skeins of yellow 771
- 4 skeins of pale yellow 773
- 2 skeins of orange 813

WORKING FROM A CHART

Each square on a needlepoint chart represents one stitch worked over one canvas intersection. The color of the yarn is shown by either a similar painted color or by a symbol in each square. As a general rule, begin in the center of the design and work outward, or stitch the main motifs first and then fill in the background.

Sewing Techniques

In this chapter we present everything you need to know for making perfect cushions. Begin by gathering the basic sewing equipment. If you sew on a fairly regular basis, you probably have most of the items in your sewing basket. The same applies for the basic techniques. If you can thread a needle and stitch a seam, then you can make up the majority of cushions offered in this book.

To help you with the needlework designs, simple embroidery and needlepoint techniques are explained in detail. Even if you've never tried the stitches, with just a little practice, you'll have them mastered to create stunning hand-worked cushions. Finally, handy reference pages include patterns for some of the featured cushions, a glossary of terms, and a few pointers on basic cushion care.

Essential sewing equipment

Check through this listing, and you may be surprised at how much sewing equipment you already have on hand. These items are easy to use and inexpensive, and they will leave you well-prepared to tackle almost any kind of cushion you choose to make.

MEASURING

Tape measure

Choose a non-stretch tape with metal ends. Each side should start and finish at opposite ends so you don't have to unwind the tape to use it.

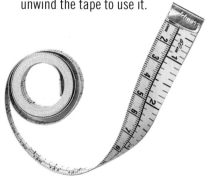

MARKING

Tailors' chalk

This is available in different colors so you can mark most fabric shades. The chalk brushes away after stitching. Keep the chalk sharp, so it will mark accurate lines.

CUTTING

Cutting out scissors

These large, strong scissors have handles that bend away from the blades. This means you can cut material flat on the table, without lifting it up. This helps prevent distortion when cutting out fabric pieces.

General sewing scissors

Use these for trimming seams and threads. Again, choose a standard size with 6-inch long blades.

Pinking shears

These scissors give a zigzag edge and are used for trimming seam allowances. Do not use them for cutting out fabric pieces, because they won't provide an accurate edge.

Needlework scissors

The sharp points of these blades are useful for snipping into tight corners.

SEWING

Pins

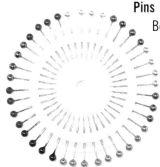

Before you begin to sew, make sure your pins are sharp and discard any blunt or damaged pins that will snag fabric. Glass-headed pins are useful when working with pile or open-weave fabrics (you also can spot them on the floor).

Needles

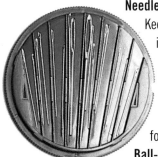

Keep a good range of needle types and sizes in your sewing basket to cover all kinds of fabrics and trims. The most useful are:

Sharps: long needles used for basting and gathering.

Betweens: small, sharp needles used for quilting and other hand-sewing.

Ball-point needles: sewing-machine needles used on knit fabric to prevent snagging.

Bodkins: blunt needles used for threading cord and elastic through casings.

SEWING MACHINES

A sewing machine is a must for the avid home sewer. First, decide what type of sewing you want to do. Machines come in a wide range of different models and almost all models do a basic lockstitch and a zigzag stitch for neatening edges and working buttonholes. More expensive machines offer embroidery

stitches. Before sewing, check your needle to make sure it is appropriate for use with your chosen fabric.

PRESSING

You'll need a good dry or steam iron, plus an ironing board. Keep a clean cloth for pressing delicate fabrics and for when you need extra steam on hard-to-press creases in natural fabrics.

THE RIGHT THREAD FOR THE JOB

Cotton thread
Smooth, strong thread with a slight sheen. Use this on cotton fabric.

Mercerized cotton thread
A treated cotton thread available in a wide range of colors. Choose all-purpose for general use and machine embroidery for finer fabrics.

Polyester thread
All-purpose thread, suitable for a variety of fabrics.

Cotton-wrapped polyester
The polyester provides strength, while the cotton provides smoothness and luster.

Silk thread
Use for stitching silk and hand-basting fine fabrics (it leaves no marks).

Buttonhole twist
Use for topstitching as well as for buttonholes. Available in synthetic or silk.

Seams and stitching

The nuts-and-bolts of successful sewing is knowing how to stitch the perfect seam. Using strong, neat seams is particularly important when making pillow cushions. The seams often are highly visible and they can take the repeated wear-and-tear a cushion receives.

PLAIN FLAT SEAM

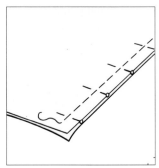

1 Place the two pieces of fabric with right sides facing and raw edges matching. Pin together across the seam line, placing pins approximately 3 inches apart, as shown. Baste along the seam line.

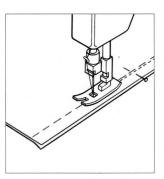

2 Position the sewing machine foot so the point of the needle is aligned with the seam line, approximately ½ inch away from the end of the seam. Work stitches in reverse to the fabric edge, then stitch forward down the complete seam. At the end of the seam, work stitches in reverse for approximately ½ inch.

3 Remove the fabric from the machine and trim off thread ends. Press the seam as it has been stitched, then press the seam open. To achieve a good seam line, press over a seam roller.

STITCHING AROUND CORNERS

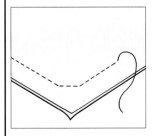

1 For neat corners, stitch on the seam line to the corner, leaving the needle in the fabric. Raise the presser foot and pivot fabric until the needle is in line with the next seam line.

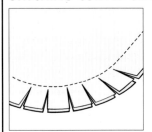

2 Lower the presser foot and continue along the seam line. On heavy fabrics it may be necessary to work stitches across the corner point, as shown.

STITCHING CURVED SEAMS

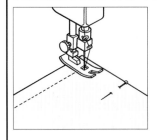

1 Stitch curved seams in the usual way. On outward curves, snip into the seam allowance so that the fabric fans out, as shown here.

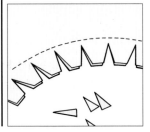

2 On inward curves, cut small notches into the seam allowance so the seam allowance can overlap on itself when the seam is pressed flat.

FRENCH SEAM

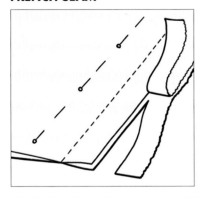

1 Place fabric pieces with wrong sides facing. Pin, baste, and stitch ¼ inch outside the finished seam line. Trim seam allowance to ¼ inch, if needed.

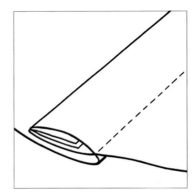

2 Refold the fabric with right sides together, pressing the seam so that it lies exactly along the edge. Pin, baste, and stitch ⅜ inch from the seamed edge.

FLAT-FELL SEAM

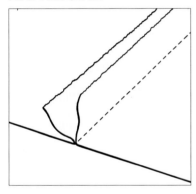

1 Stitch fabric pieces together with right sides facing, using a ½-inch seam. Press seam open, then over to one side. Trim inner seam allowance to a scant ¼ inch.

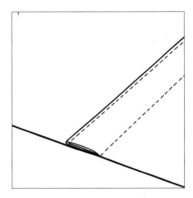

2 Press the wider seam allowance in half, encasing the narrower seam allowance. Press the seam down to the fabric. Pin, baste, then edgestitch along the folded edge.

PIPED SEAM

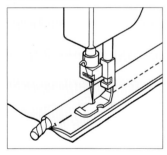

1 Make up a length of covered piping cord. Lay the piping cord along the seam line of the first fabric piece, with the cord facing inwards and raw edges matching the raw fabric edges; pin and baste in place. Using a piping foot on the machine, stitch along the seam line.

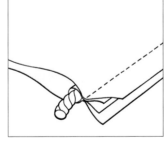

2 Place the second fabric piece against the first piece, right sides together, with the piping in between and matching raw edges. Pin, baste, and stitch along the seam line again, using the previous stitching line as a guide.

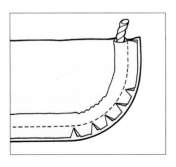

3 On curved seams, snip into the piping seam allowance at regular intervals and around the curved edge.

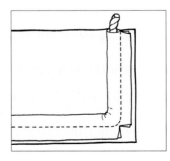

4 At sharp corners, snip into the piping seam allowance from the corner point to the stitching line to help spread the fabric at the corner.

Hand-stitching

The following are the basic hand-stitching techniques you'll need in order to tackle a full range of cushions.

GATHERING FABRIC BY HAND

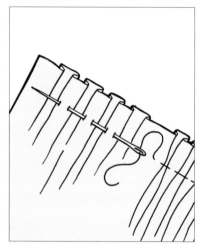

1 Work from the right side, with thread approximately 8 inches longer than the length to be gathered. Work a few running stitches at a time before pulling the thread through the fabric.

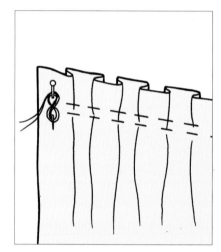

2 Work a second row in the same way, ¼ inch above the first row. Pull up both threads together to form even gathers. Stitch over the threads as before.

BACKSTITCH

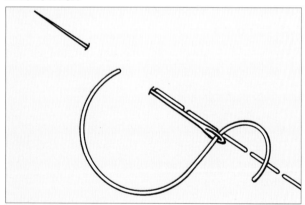

Work from right to left. For the first stitch, bring the threaded needle up through the fabric and then take it back down one stitch length to the right of the point where the thread emerged. Now bring the needle up through the fabric, one stitch length in front (and to the left) of the first stitch. Push the needle down through fabric at the beginning of the first stitch. Continue in this manner to the end of the seam.

FEATHER STITCH

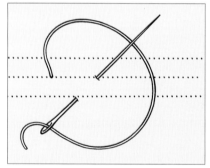

1 Make the stitch by taking the needle diagonally through the fabric left to right and below the thread, making a loop.

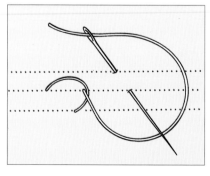

2 Take the needle through the fabric again, working right to left and making a loop. Continue alternating stitches.

HERRINGBONE STITCH

A strong stitch used for hems, holding raw edges, and joining lengths of batting. Work from left to right with the needle pointing towards the left. Secure the thread with a couple of backstitches. Take a stitch from right to left in one fabric, then take the needle up across the edge and take another stitch from right to left in the second. Continue, forming evenly spaced cross-stitches.

RUNNING STITCH

Use this for gathering fabric. Begin with a couple of backstitches, then work from right to left, weaving the needle in and out of the fabric and taking small, evenly spaced stitches.

SLIP-STITCH

An almost invisible stitch used to hold two folded edges together (for example, across a cushion opening). Work from right to left. Begin with a knot and secure it inside the fold of the hem. Bring the thread out of one folded edge and slide inside the opposite folded edge. Come out of this fold and repeat.

STABSTITCH

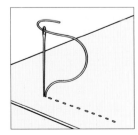

A useful stitch to hold two pieces of fabric together with almost invisible stitches, such as for appliqué. Work from right to left with the needle in a vertical position, taking tiny stitches on the right side of the fabric. On the wrong side, the stitches will be slightly longer.

BASTING

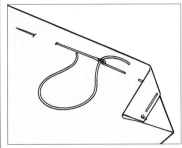

Work with a single or double thread and begin with a knot. Work through the fabric, making stitches and gaps approximately $\frac{3}{8}$- to $\frac{3}{4}$-inch long. At the opposite end, take one backstitch and trim off the thread. To remove basting stitches, simply snip off the knot and pull the thread out of the fabric.

DIAGONAL BASTING

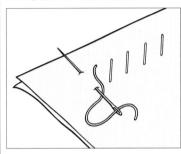

This is the best way to hold two slippery fabrics together and to secure pleats or layers of batting to a fabric. With the needle pointing from right to left, take horizontal stitches through the fabric, forming a row of slanting stitches. Work vertically or horizontally across the fabric.

LADDER STITCH

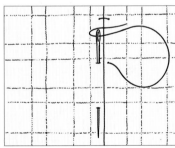

Use this to match two patterned pieces of fabric together. The stitch is worked on the right side of the fabric. Press under one seam allowance and pin over the opposite seam allowance, exactly matching the pattern design. Working from the right side, take a $\frac{1}{4}$-inch long stitch through the folded edge. Bring out the needle, take it vertically across the seam line and slide it under the flat fabric for $\frac{1}{4}$-inch. Continue stitching ladder stitches across the join in this way. When the seam is complete, simply fold the fabric with right sides together and stitch along the seam line.

Embroidery stitches

Illustrated here are all the embroidery and needlepoint stitches you will need to make the hand-worked cushion covers in this book (see pages 72–79). With a little imagination, it is easy to create attractive covers of your own design.

CHAIN STITCH

This can be stitched in closely worked rows to cover areas of a design.

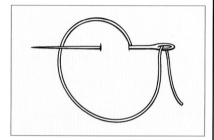

1 Bring the needle out of the fabric, then take a stitch, starting at the original point.

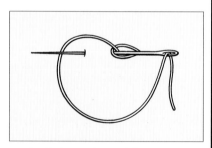

2 Pull through the fabric over the working thread, forming a loop.

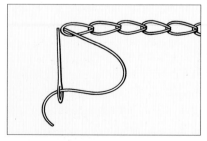

3 Make the next stitch from this position to form a linking chain.

DETACHED CHAIN STITCH (LAZY DAISY STITCH)

This stitch is the same as chain stitch but is worked as a separate stitch.

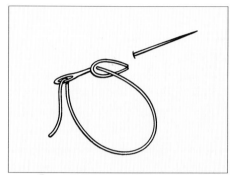

1 Form a loop in exactly the same way as for the chain stitch.

2 Once the chain is formed, take a small backstitch over the end, then take the needle under the fabric to the position for the next stitch.

SATIN STITCH

This fills in an area with long, straight stitches.

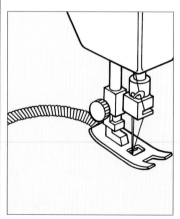

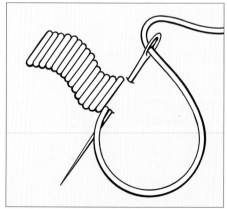

1 Work a straight stitch from left to right across the fabric by machine or by hand.

2 Continue placing each stitch exactly beside the previous stitch, taking care to keep the worked edge straight and the stitches even.

SEED STITCH

Use in groups or scattered all over a design.

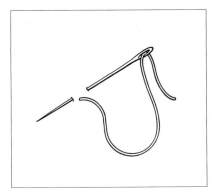

1 Bring the needle out of the fabric and take a tiny back stitch.

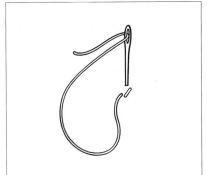

2 Repeat, placing two stitches side by side before moving on to the position of the next stitch.

STEM STITCH

Stem stitch usually is used to outline areas of a design. Work from left to right.

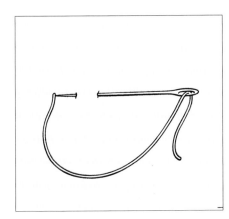

1 Bring the needle out of the fabric and take a stitch, bringing the needle up halfway between the first stitch.

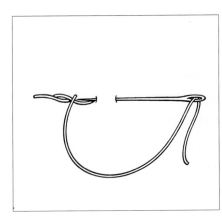

2 Repeat this sequence, keeping the thread below the needle to form neat, overlapping stitches.

HALF CROSS-STITCH

Work this needlepoint stitch in two movements, with the guiding hand below the canvas and the other hand above the canvas. Work individual stitches from left to right.

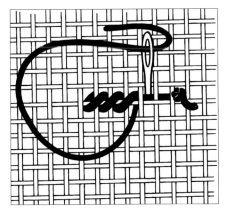

1 Come out the canvas and take a diagonal stitch from lower left to upper right over one intersection. Take next stitch to left of first stitch.

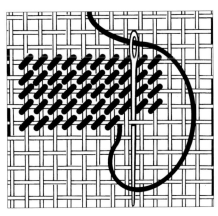

2 Work the second row in reverse, or simply turn the canvas and work back the same way.

Patterns

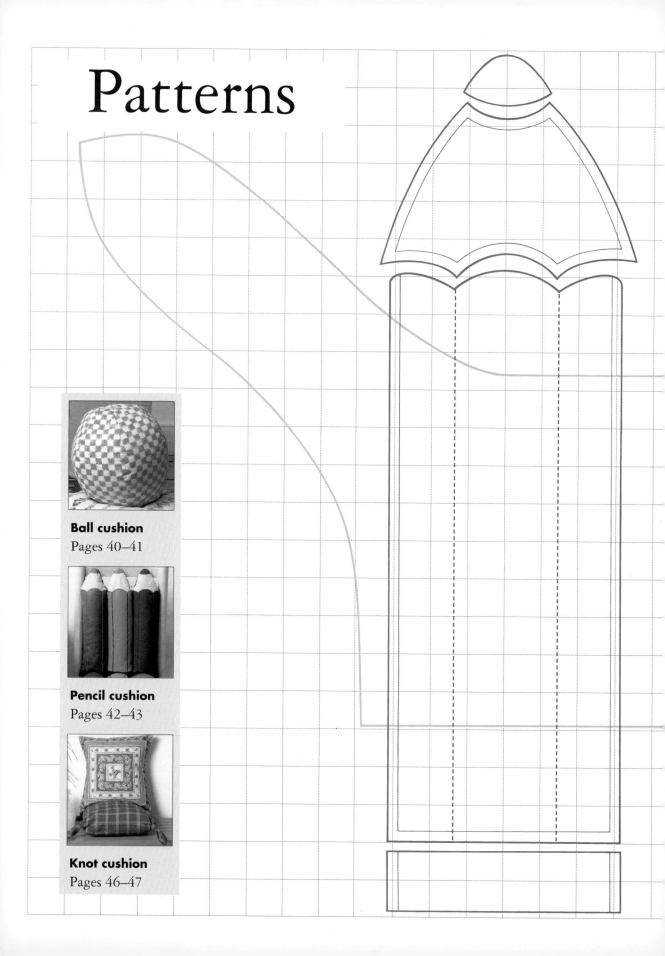

Ball cushion
Pages 40–41

Pencil cushion
Pages 42–43

Knot cushion
Pages 46–47

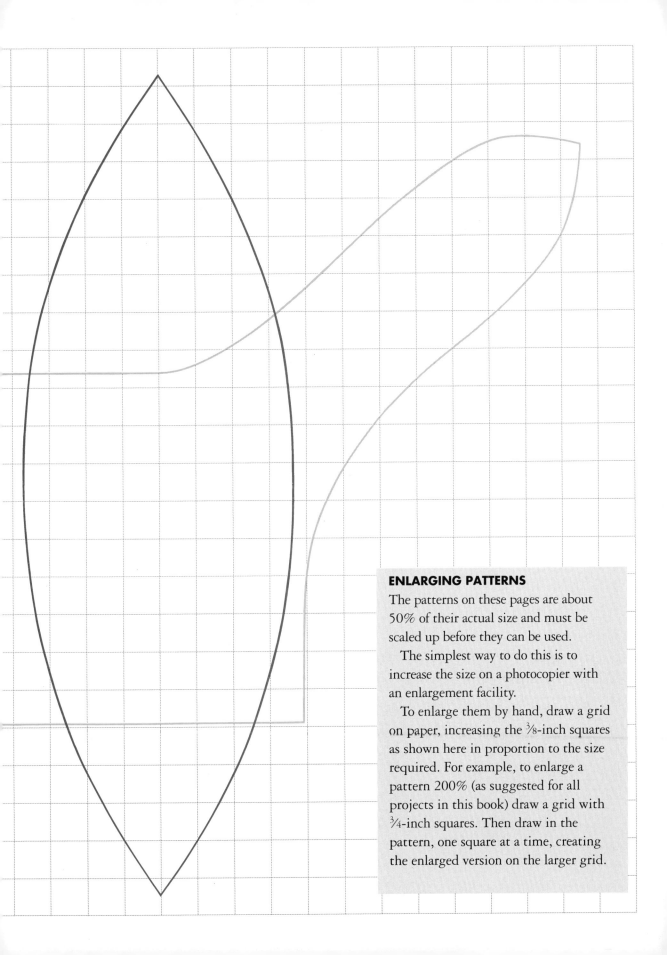

ENLARGING PATTERNS

The patterns on these pages are about 50% of their actual size and must be scaled up before they can be used.

The simplest way to do this is to increase the size on a photocopier with an enlargement facility.

To enlarge them by hand, draw a grid on paper, increasing the ³⁄₈-inch squares as shown here in proportion to the size required. For example, to enlarge a pattern 200% (as suggested for all projects in this book) draw a grid with ³⁄₄-inch squares. Then draw in the pattern, one square at a time, creating the enlarged version on the larger grid.

Glossary

Appliqué
A design created when one fabric or shape is applied to another.

Batting
Bonded fabric, in various thicknesses, used to add depth and warmth to another fabric.

Bias
The diagonal line of fabric formed when the lengthwise grain of the fabric is folded to meet the crosswise grain of the fabric.

Bias binding
Strip of fabric cut on the bias and used to bind curved edges.

Brocade
Distinctive fabric with differently woven areas forming a raised pattern.

Calico
Strong, inexpensive, woven cotton fabric.

Casing
A channel formed by two parallel rows of stitching.

Crewelwork
Embroidery using wool thread on a fabric background.

Devoré velvet
Velvet fabric chemically treated to 'devour' some of the pile, leaving a pattern.

Embroidery hoop
Two close fitting wooden or plastic hoops that hold taut a piece of embroidery while it is worked.

Gathering
A running stitch or machine stitch that is pulled up to regulate the fullness of a piece of fabric.

Grain
The direction in which the fibers run in a length of fabric.

Gusset
Strip of fabric added between a top and bottom piece to give depth.

Miter
A corner seam that neatly joins two hems at right angles to each other.

Muslin
Inexpensive cotton fabric, available unbleached or bleached.

Needlepoint
Wool or yarn embroidery worked over a sturdy canvas or even-weave fabric.

Piping
Piping is a folded strip of fabric, inserted into a seam as an edging. It can be flat or form a covering for piping cord.

Pivot
To create a sharp corner by leaving the needle in the fabric and turning the fabric.

Poplin
Popular hard-wearing cotton fabric with a slight sheen.

Pre-shrinking
Laundering fabrics and trimmings before assembling them into finished items to prevent shrinkage.

Quilting
A decorative method of joining two pieces of fabric with a batting center.

Seam allowance
The amount of fabric allowed for stitching seams—measuring from $\frac{1}{4}$ inch to $\frac{5}{8}$ inch wide.

Seam line
The line designated for stitching the seam.

Selvage
The non-fraying, tightly-woven edge running down both side edges of a length of fabric.

Tapestry frame
Wooden frame used to hold a piece of canvas or fabric taut while embroidering.

Tension
The balance and tightness of the needle thread and bobbin thread on a sewing machine that combine to create the perfect stitch.

Thread count
The number of threads per inch in the warp and weft threads of needlepoint canvas or embroidery fabrics.

Tucks
Narrow, stitched folds of fabric that provide a tailored, decorative feature.

Zigzag stitch
Machine stitch used as a decorative stitch and used to neaten seams by preventing fabric threads from raveling.

CUSHION CARE
• Shake out and air cushion forms regularly.
• Wash feather cushion forms in warm, sudsy water and rinse well. Shake forms occasionally as they dry. Wash synthetic-filled forms by hand or machine and tumble dry. Do not dry-clean forms—the filling can absorb toxic cleaning-fluid fumes. Foam forms can be washed gently in warm, sudsy water. Rinse, squeeze well, and dry in a warm place, away from direct heat to avoid fumes from the foam.
• Treat any stains as they occur, then wash the cover.
• When washing covers, close zippers and fastenings.
• Press covers while slightly damp to iron out any creases.
• If you are unaware of a cover's fiber content, have it dry-cleaned.

Index

Meredith® Press
An imprint of Meredith® Books

Do-It-Yourself Decorating
Step-by-Step Pillows & Cushions
Editor: Vicki L. Ingham
Technical Editor: Laura H. Collins
Contributing Designer: Jeff Harrison
Copy Chief: Angela K. Renkoski
Electronic Production Coordinator: Paula Forest
Editorial and Design Assistants: Barbara A. Suk, Jennifer Norris, Karen Schirm
Production Director: Douglas M. Johnston
Production Manager: Pam Kvitne
Assistant Prepress Manager: Marjorie J. Schenkelberg

Meredith® Books
Editor in Chief: James D. Blume
Design Director: Matt Strelecki
Managing Editor: Gregory H. Kayko
Executive Editor, Shelter Books: Denise L. Caringer

Director, Sales & Marketing, Retail: Michael A. Peterson
Director, Sales & Marketing, Special Markets: Rita McMullen
Director, Sales & Marketing, Home & Garden Center Channel: Ray Wolf
Director, Operations: Valerie Wiese
Vice President, General Manager: Jamie L. Martin

Meredith Publishing Group
President, Publishing Group: Christopher M. Little
Vice President, Consumer Marketing & Development: Hal Oringer
Meredith Corporation
Chairman and Chief Executive Officer: William T. Kerr

Chairman of the Executive Committee: E.T. Meredith III

Cover photograph: George Wright
First published 1998 by Haynes Publishing
Sparkford, Nr Yeovil, Somerset BA22 7JJ, UK

All of us at Meredith® Books are dedicated to providing you with information and ideas you
need to enhance your home. We welcome your comments and suggestions about this book on
Pillows & Cushions. Write to us at: Meredith® Books, Do-It-Yourself Editorial Department,
RW–206, 1716 Locust St., Des Moines, IA 50309–3023.